# THE
# POLITICAL HISTORY OF VIRGINIA DURING THE RECONSTRUCTION

Series XXII Nos. 6-7-8

JOHNS HOPKINS UNIVERSITY STUDIES

IN

HISTORICAL AND POLITICAL SCIENCE

(Edited by H. B. Adams, 1882-1901)



# THE POLITICAL HISTORY OF VIRGINIA DURING THE RECONSTRUCTION

BY

HAMILTON JAMES ECKENRODE



GLOUCESTER, MASS.

PETER SMITH

1966

# CONTENTS

# PREFACE.

This monograph does not attempt to deal with the economic, social and constitutional features of the reconstruction. The investigation is chiefly concerned with political parties. It demonstrates the following facts:

(1) The Alexandria government formed the nucleus of the Republican party in Virginia, and reconstructive measures were attempted at Alexandria before the end of the war.

(2) President Johnson wished to restore the Southern States to their former position, consequently his policy should not be called reconstruction, the term applying properly to the action of Congress.

(3) The Republican party in Virginia was for the most part opposed to unlimited negro suffrage, until the Philadelphia convention of 1866, when "manhood" suffrage became a party measure.

(4) The opposition of the Virginia Republicans to Johnson's State government and their adverse testimony before the reconstruction committee played a considerable part in occasioning the reconstruction of Virginia.

(5) The Freedmen's Bureau and the Union League were the agencies which drew the freedmen into the Republican party.

(6) In the beginning of the reconstruction a considerable and influential part of the conservative people, chiefly Whigs, attempted to unite with the blacks in the Republican party, but were repulsed by them; in fact, the extreme radical attitude of the freedmen was one of the chief causes of the united opposition of the whites to negro suffrage.

(7) The policy of the Republicans in the constitutional convention of 1868 was to make the negro a full citizen by granting him suffrage, the right to office-holding and jury-service; to provide him with education; and to give him the chance of attaining economic independence.

(8) The restoration of Virginia was due to the joint action of the conservatives and of the Republicans hostile to extreme radicalism.

I wish to express my thanks to Dr. J. M. Vincent and especially to Dr. J. C. Ballagh for assistance in preparing this work; and also to friends in Virginia for the loan of valuable material, for oral evidence and for suggestions.

# THE POLITICAL RECONSTRUCTION OF VIRGINIA.

## CHAPTER I.

### The Alexandria Government.

It is a notable fact that the border Confederate States were divided against themselves, the line of separation generally following the chief mountain ranges. This was the case in Kentucky and Tennessee. In Virginia conditions were similar. The Blue Ridge was the natural division line of the State. To the east lay old Virginia, a country of slave-holders and plantations; the west was largely divided into small farms and the slaves were few. There had long been a difference of interests between the sections and a considerable political antagonism. The west, almost ever since the Revolution, had agitated for reform in the unequal system of representation which gave the east many more delegates in proportion to the white population than the west. In the constitutional convention of 1829-30, the question of representation held the chief place, but no satisfactory basis was decided upon, for the westerners wished to limit representation strictly to the white population.[1]

The constitution did not prove satisfactory and in 1850-51 another convention was held, which arranged a compromise, giving the control of the house of delegates to the west on a basis of white representation, and the majority in

[1] Representation in Virginia, p. 32 et seq. Debates of the Convention of 1829-30.

the senate to the east upon the basis of taxation.[2] This arrangement lasted until the Civil War.

The Virginia convention, which had been elected for the purpose of considering the question of secession, passed an ordinance to that effect on April 17, 1861. The delegates from the northwest counties voted solidly against it, and almost immediately upon the reception of the news of its passage the people of the trans-Alleghany country began to prepare for separate action. At a meeting in Harrison county, the disaffected citizens appointed delegates to a convention, which was advertised to meet at Wheeling on May 13, 1861. The other northern counties were invited to attend.[3] Accordingly delegates were appointed to the convention by counties, towns, villages and neighborhoods. Little form was used, and the appointments in many cases were entirely irregular.[4]

This anti-secession convention assembled at Wheeling on May 11, 1861. It soon adjourned, however, owing to dissatisfaction with the unequal method of representation employed, which was inadequate for the election of responsible men. Arrangements were made for calling another convention in June, to be composed of the State senators, members of the house of delegates and delegates double the number of the latter, who should be elected by the counties.[5] The May convention, before adjournment, passed ordinances condemning secession and declaring the intention of the convention to defend the Constitution of the United States.

The second convention met at Wheeling, on June 11, 1861. The first resolution adopted bound each member to take an oath to support the Constitution of the United States, "anything in the ordinance of secession . . . to the contrary notwithstanding."

---

[2] Representation in Virginia, p. 60 et seq.
[3] A general invitation to the whole State was not extended.
[4] Code of Virginia (1873).
[5] Speech of Senator Van Winkle in the U. S. Senate, April 21, 1864, p. 17.

The refusal to accede to the ordinance of secession cut off the northwestern counties from the Confederate east. It was now decided to erect a new government in Virginia, entirely independent of the regular State administration, and a declaration was issued to justify this radical step. It said: "The true purpose of all government is to promote the welfare and provide for the protection and security of the governed, and when any form or organization of government proves inadequate for, or subversive of this purpose, it is the right, it is the duty of the latter to alter or abolish it."[6] After thus expressing the right of revolution, the convention proceeded to organize a new State administration. An ordinance declared vacant the offices of governor, lieutenant-governor and attorney-general and all other offices held by secessionists. New officers were elected by the convention for the term of six months. The governorship was given to Francis Harrison Peirpont, of Marion county, who had taken an active part in organizing the movement.

The new State administration so organized styled itself the "Restored Government of Virginia," entirely ignoring the existence of the legal State government at Richmond. While the supporters of the new administration recognized its revolutionary character, they held that they were justified by the circumstances, and even adduced authority for their action.[7]

The general assembly of the "Restored Government"

---

[6] Van Winkle's Speech, p. 18, and Constitution and Acts of Virginia (Alexandria), p. 5.

[7] Journal House of Delegates (Alexandria), 1863-4, p. 9. First and foremost, President Lincoln, when appealed to by Governor Peirpont, acknowledged the validity of the act and sent military aid. The Federalist and the Supreme Court case of Luther vs. Borden were also quoted. The chief authority was derived from the fourth section of the fourth article of the Constitution of the United States, which reads: "The United States shall guarantee to every State in this Union, a republican form of government, and protect each of them against invasion," etc.

This clause, really designed to protect State interests, was used in the war period with a most remarkable freedom of interpretation.

met at Wheeling in extra session on July 1, 1861. It was composed of former members of the Virginia legislature from the northwest counties, and of new members elected in the spring. The western section of the State was by this time fully committed to the Union cause. Federal troops had early occupied that region and carried it away from the Confederacy; citizens of Union sentiments were in full control of political affairs, and the assembly took measures to support the Washington government. It voted $175,000 for the equipment of soldiers[8] and authorized the governor to borrow $200,000.[9] Counties and corporations were also given power to appropriate money for the public expense.[10] Vigorous action was taken against the Confederates of the western counties. Offices were declared vacant, if the oath of allegiance to the Federal government was not taken,[11] and persons leaving within twenty days for the Confederate army should be considered non-residents and might be proceeded against by process of attachment.[12] The assembly passed an ordinance on August 9, 1861, which declared the proceedings of the State secession convention null and void.[13]

The assembly now prepared to take the final step of alienation from Confederate Virginia. The west, as we have seen, had long differed politically and economically from the east. Separation might have been effected under peaceful conditions, but the beginning of hostilities severed the last ties between the sections. The counter-movement of the west naturally went on in its development and the assembly began to make arrangements for the erection of another State out of the territory of Virginia. An act was passed on August 29, 1861, providing for the formation of a new State, to be called Kanawha, and for the election of delegates to form a constitution for it. A provision was also made that the State of Kanawha should take upon

[8] Constitution and Acts (Alexandria), 1861-5, p. 4. [9] Ibid.
[10] Constitution and Acts (Alexandria), 1861-5, p. 13. [11] Ibid., p. 7.
[12] Ibid., p. 25. [13] Constitution and Acts (Alexandria), p. 53.

itself a just proportion of the debt of Virginia as it stood before the beginning of the war.[14]

At the regular session of the legislature on December 2, 1861, a series of sweeping measures were adopted. Most striking was the revolutionary plan for the partition of Virginia. The assembly was not satisfied with having divided the State; it was now bent on a complete dismemberment of the Old Dominion. An act was passed on February 3, 1862, by the legislature which claimed to represent Virginia, providing for a vote in Accomac and Northampton counties on the question of annexation to Maryland.[15] The plan for partition was continued at the extra session of the legislature, which met on May 6, 1862. On May 13, an act was passed giving the consent of Virginia to the formation of a new State out of her own territory, and also consenting to the incorporation of the counties of Berkeley, Jefferson and Frederick in the State, when they should vote to ratify the constitution. West Virginia,[16] not satisfied with this liberal share of territory, at the next regular session of the legislature on December 4, 1862, prepared a very comprehensive scheme of aggrandizement. The consent of Virginia was given to a measure that would have proven her ruin, if the politicians at Wheeling had been able to enforce it; that is, the incorporation in West Virginia[17] of the counties of Berkeley, Tazewell, Bland, Giles, Craig, Buchanan, Wise, Russell, Scott, Lee, Highland, Bath, Frederick, Jefferson, Clarke, Loudoun, Fairfax, Alexandria, Prince William, Shenandoah, Warren, Page and Rockingham—twenty-three in all. By this partition Virginia would have been deprived of most of her western and all of her northern counties.

West Virginia was now prepared to enter upon an independent career, and Governor Peirpont's "Restored Government" was no longer needed there. Accordingly he re-

[14] Constitution and Acts, p. 93. [15] Constitution and Acts.
[16] This name was preferred to that of Kanawha.
[17] Constitution and Acts, p. 11.

moved to Alexandria, which now became the seat of a Union administration in Virginia. Peirpont had declined to be a candidate for office in West Virginia, preferring to continue as the head of the Virginia administration. After the separation of West Virginia, the Peirpont government was reduced to a little strip of territory in northern and eastern Virginia within the Union lines. The sentiment of the people in Alexandria differed greatly from that of the people of Wheeling. A majority of the West Virginians supported the Union cause, although there was a very considerable Confederate element; consequently the government of West Virginia was founded upon popular approval. But in the country along the Potomac, where Peirpont set up his régime, by far the greater part of the inhabitants were loyal to the Confederacy and the regular State government at Richmond. The Peirpont administration at Alexandria existed only in the shadow of the Federal armies and would have been summarily expelled by the people but for them. It suited the policy of the Federal government to recognize Peirpont's pretentions, but it must not be thought from this recognition that the Alexandria government was based upon the consent and approval of the governed.

That government held sway from the summer of 1863 until the spring of 1865. It comprised the counties of Alexandria and Fairfax on the Potomac, the Eastern Shore and the country around Norfolk. It is true that other counties sent delegates to the legislature, but they were the scenes of active warfare, and paid no taxes to the Alexandria government, so that they can hardly be said to have formed a part of it. Fairfax county, the chief territorial possession of the Peirpont régime, was represented both in the Alexandria legislature and in the legislature at Richmond.

Soon after Governor Peirpont's arrival in Alexandria, arrangements were made to hold elections for State, city and county officers under the new government. A vote was also to be taken in several counties upon changing allegiance to West Virginia. At a convention at Alexandria on May 14, 1863, Peirpont was renominated for governor, Edmond Pendleton for lieutenant-governor and S. Ferguson Beach for attorney-general.[18] The last two nominees resigned and were replaced by G. O. Wunder and T. R. Bowden. Wunder, however, although nominated at Alexandria with Peirpont, was not elected. Peirpont received 3,755 votes, probably the whole number cast, as he had no open opposition. E. L. C. Cooper was elected lieutenant-governor with 2,361 votes, and T. R. Bowden, attorney-general, with 2,743, "being a large majority of the votes cast over all other candidates for these offices."[19] In the Seventh Congressionial district, the only one holding a Congressional election, B. M. Kitchen received 911 votes and Lewis McKenzie, 714.[20] Members of the general assembly were also elected on an extremely small vote.

On the important question of changing allegiance to West Virginia, Berkeley county gave 645 votes in the affirmative and 7 in the negative. It is not apparent what the real sentiment of Jefferson county was, but it was probably opposed to separation from Virginia. The total vote in that county was 337 out of an average of 2000; the majority was for incorporation in West Virginia. In Fairfax county 53 or 54 votes were cast in favor of annexation, 25 against it.

The election was held in the midst of war and confusion. The district was constantly occupied by the contending armies and was the scene of almost daily fighting. A great

---

[18] Alexandria Gazette, May 14-15, 1863.
Twenty delegates were appointed to this convention from Alexandria and there were also delegates present from Norfolk, Spottsylvania, Berkeley, Loudoun, Fairfax and Fauquier. Few of them really represented constituents, as on the motion of Lewis McKenzie of Alexandria, any person present from the adjoining counties was admitted as a delegate.

[19] Alexandria Gazette, December 4, 1863.

[20] McKenzie vs. Kitchen, House Documents, 38th Congress, 1st session, No. 12.

part of the inhabitants had fled to safer regions. Election forms were very elastic,[21] consequently the election was confused and utterly irregular and representative of a mere handful of the population. Jefferson and Berkeley counties, while voting for admission to West Virginia, elected members to the Virginia (Alexandria) legislature. In the Congressional election, B. M. Kitchen received 91 votes, a plurality. The whole district was soon afterwards occupied by Confederate troops, but as soon as they had retired, Lewis McKenzie, the rival candidate for Congress, filed papers for a contest.[22] Congress, however, refused to seat either candidate.

Governor Peirpont, some time afterwards, sent certificates of the election in the two counties to the governor of West Virginia. Berkeley was thereupon nominally incorporated in the latter State on August 5, 1863, and Jefferson, on November 2, 1863. Although thus duly annexed to West Virginia, the allegiance of the counties remained uncertain for a considerable length of time. The members of the general assembly elected from Berkeley and Jefferson seem to have applied for admission to the Virginia assembly in December, 1863, for we find the Virginia State Journal in January, 1864, objecting to their admission to the Alexandria legislature.[23] The allegiance of Berkeley and Jeffer-

---

[21] McKenzie vs. Kitchen, House Documents, 38th Congress, 1st session, No. 12. In Jefferson county, only two polls were open for voting; in Loudoun, apparently two; in Prince William, only one. Many votes were cast by men of short residence in the State.

[22] He claimed that his vote was the next largest, and would be largest if the vote of Berkeley county were excluded, which he urged be done on the ground that Berkeley had voted for incorporation with West Virginia and so ceased to be a part of Virginia. The majority of the committee of Congress decided adversely to both claimants, declaring that only a minority of the people of the Seventh District had voted on the election. Polls were open in only six of the eleven counties and only in parts of several of the six.

[23] McKenzie vs. Kitchen, House Misc. Documents, 38th Congress, 1st session, No. 12.

Alexandria Gazette, January 7, 1864. The State Journal said: "The position of our State is already in a strange condition and nothing should be done to befog the people more than they are now befogged." The members were not admitted, but, nevertheless, no one was certain whether the counties belonged to Virginia or West Virginia.

son remained uncertain through the war, and together they formed a senatorial district under the Alexandria constitution of 1864. In December, 1865, when the government had been removed to Richmond and a new legislature representative of the whole of Virginia had been electted, the consent of the State to the cession of the two counties was withdrawn. This repeal, however, was disregarded and Congress passed an act on March 2, 1866, giving its consent to the incorporation of Jefferson and Berkeley in West Virginia. They were thereafter included in that State. One of the first acts of Virginia in 1870 was to bring the case before the Supreme Court. But the decision went against her and West Virginia retained the counties.[24]

The legislature of the "Restored Government of Virginia" held its first meeting at Alexandria on December 7, 1863, in the chambers of the city council. Six senators were present, representing Fairfax, Alexandria, Accomac, Norfolk, Loudoun counties and Norfolk city. Norfolk, Loudoun, Alexandria, Northampton and Prince William counties were represented by seven delegates. J. Madison Downey of Loudoun was elected speaker of the house of delegates.

This tiny legislature, representing the Virginia Unionists, naturally had few regular questions of legislation to decide. Its chief work was to provide for the amendment of the constitution in regard to slavery. "Everybody," said Governor Peirpont in his message, "loyal or disloyal, concedes that slavery in the State is doomed. Then acting upon this concession, call a convention of loyal delegates,

---

[24] Supreme Court Reports, 1870, Virginia vs. West Virginia. Virginia argued that as she had withdrawn her consent to the cession by an act of December 8, 1865, and as Congress had not ratified the cession till March 2, 1866, therefore the compact was void. Furthermore that the election was a fraud and for this reason Virginia had withdrawn her consent. The court decided that the State of Virginia had given her consent to the transfer, that the governor had certified to the election returns, and that as no specific charge of fraud had been made, it would not go beneath the returns. The case was, therefore, dismissed. Justices Davis, Clifford and Field dissented on the ground that Virginia had withdrawn her consent before the Congressional ratification.

to alter the State constitution in this particular, and declare slavery and involuntary servitude, except for crime, to be forever abolished in the State."[25]

In accordance with the governor's instructions, a bill providing for a constitutional convention was introduced and passed, not without opposition, Reuben Johnson denouncing the haste with which the body "undertook to legislate for the calling together of a dozen men to perform one of the most momentous acts in the history of the State."[26] In the house of delegates, the vote was 7 to 4 in favor of the convention bill; one vote was against in the senate.

The temper of the legislature was generally indicative of the new feeling of the times, but no radical measures were taken. Job Hawxhurst introduced a bill providing for the repeal of those sections of the code of 1860 which prohibited the education of negroes.[27] This, which seems to have been the most radical bill introduced in the legislature, failed to pass. E. R. Birch, on January 15, 1864, brought up a bill for the relief of the slave-holders of Northampton county. The phrase in the bill, "their slave property," was struck out as unacceptable, and the clause, "such slaves as they have been deprived of," inserted in place of it. This bill, however, was defeated,[28] and its defeat showed how the sentiment of Unionists had changed as to slavery.

The legislature met for its second session on December 5, 1864. Three new members were sworn in, but no new counties sent representatives. J. Madison Downey was re-elected speaker and George Tucker, clerk of the house of delegates. The governor's message was a long and important document and indicated the changes of opinion

[25] Peirpont went on to say that the emancipation proclamation had freed all the slaves in the state except in a few counties. But the Virginia laws recognized slavery and there would be a conflict of authorities, and "rebels glory in strife." The governor believed that the Federal government would recompense loyal slave-holders.

[26] Alexandria Gazette, December 18, 1863.

[27] Journal House of Delegates, 1863-4, p. 46.

[28] Journal House of Delegates, 1863-4, p. 53.

that the war was bringing about. Peirpont gave his views upon the all-important negro question. He congratulated the constitutional convention, which had met in the spring, on the abolition of slavery in Virginia, and advocated sweeping changes in the laws concerning negroes. The act prescribing different punishments for blacks, should, he said, be altered in accordance with the amended constitution, as well as the law for apprenticing them. The law prohibiting the education of negroes should be abolished. Peirpont hesitated to advocate the extension of the privilege of testifying in courts to negroes, on account of the strong prejudice against it. His language was, on the whole, very moderate.[29] He advised the legalizing of the marital relations of negroes, and, most important, the establishment of public schools, which should be supported by the sale of lands condemned for taxes.[30]

Notwithstanding the governor's advice, no acts of great importance passed the legislature. Two Senators were elected to represent Virginia in Congress—Joseph Segar to fill the vacancy caused by the death of Lemuel J. Bowden, and John C. Underwood for the full term beginning March 4, 1865. Neither of them, however, was admitted to a seat in the Senate. Bills providing for the introduction of negro testimony in legal proceedings and for the establishment of free public schools were introduced in the legislature, but were not passed. On February 9, 1865, the assembly ratified the thirteenth amendment to the Constitution of the United States. It adjourned on March 7. This was the last session at Alexandria. The next and final meeting was held in the city of Richmond on June 19, 1865.

The chief work of the Alexandria government was the

---

[29] "The disruption of the social system of Virginia has been sudden The almost violent release of the slave population of the State from the bonds of the master, is an experiment in human progress that is gigantic in its magnitude and momentous in its results to mankind. This act produced fearful apprehensions in the minds of the best and wisest as to its immediate consequences."

[30] Journal House of Delegates, 1864-5.

framing of a new constitution for Virginia which should supercede the one of 1851 and express the Union sentiments of the Potomac legislators. Nominations of delegates to the constitutional convention were made in January, 1864. By the terms of the act of the legislature, any voter in the State who had not adhered by word or act to the Confederacy since September 1, 1861, might be chosen a member of the convention; all loyal citizens, who had not given aid or comfort to the Confederacy since January 1, 1863, possessed the right to vote. On account of the very small number of counties within the limits of the Alexandria government, it was necessary that each county should be largely represented in the convention. Accordingly, a peculiar system of representation was adopted, by which the districts that elected State senators, as well as the individual counties, elected delegates to the convention.[31]

The election of members to the constitutional convention took place on January 22, 1864.[32] The people showed very little interest and but few of them voted; the great majority were Confederate in sympathy. In Fairfax county, 208 votes were cast, the most of them for John Hawxhurst. In Alexandria, S. R. Birch received 94 votes as the "senatorial" delegate and W. L. Penn, 92 as "county" delegate. Messrs. Henshaw, Downey and Giver were elected from Loudoun county on a very small vote, and in the Norfolk region and the Eastern Shore it was correspondingly light. A handful of Union men made the nominations and did the voting.

The convention met at Alexandria on February 13, 1864.

---

[31] Alexandria Gazette, Jan. 13 and 14, 1864. A nominating meeting was held at Alexandria on January 12, 1864. S. F. Beach was nominated as the "Senatorial" delegate from Alexandria and William L. Penn in the "County Convention," receiving ten votes as against five for Jefferson Tacey. It will be seen how very few people participated in the nomination. No delegates had been appointed to the convention from Alexandria county, although Fairfax had sent her quota. In the absence of regular delegates from Alexandria, men were appointed on the spot by the chairman to act as such. The whole proceeding of this meeting was very informal.

[32] Alexandria Gazette, January 22-23, 1864.

Twelve counties were represented by fifteen delegates.[33] Le Roy G. Edwards was elected president and W. J. Cowing, secretary. The convention made a number of changes in the constitution of 1851. In consequence of the separation of West Virginia, a redistricting of the State was necessary. It will be noted in this connection that Jefferson and Berkeley counties together formed the thirty-fourth senatorial district under the new constitution, although they had been declared a part of West Virginia some months before.[34] The number of judges of the Supreme Court was reduced from five to three;[35] these should now be nominated by the governor and confirmed by the legislature. The time of residence of voters was made one year instead of three as formerly, in order that newcomers might be speedily enfranchised. On the other hand, the convention adopted disfranchising articles for the benefit of the Confederates. Persons who held offices, civil or military, under the "rebel" government of Virginia, except county offices, were disfranchised. Also persons offering to vote were required to take oath to support the Constitution of the United States as the supreme law of the land; to support the "Restored Government of Virginia," and to swear that the voter had not willingly aided the "rebellion" since January 1, 1864.[36]

The most important amendment was the article relating to the abolition of slavery and the regulation of the negroes. Clause nineteen of article four declared that "Slavery and involuntary servitude (except for crime) is hereby abolished and prohibited in the State forever." County courts were empowered to apprentice negro children on the same terms

---

[33] Appleton's Annual Cyclopædia, 1864, p. 809. The counties represented were: Alexandria and Fairfax by W. L. Penn, S. Ferguson Beach and John Hawxhurst; Norfolk city and county by Dr. L. W. Webb and W. W. Wing; Portsmouth city and county by G. R. Bouch, P. G. Thomas and Le Roy G. Edwards; Loudoun by Dr. J. J. Henshaw, J. Madison Downey and E. R. Giver; York, Warwick, Elizabeth City, Charles City, James City and New Kent by T. S. Tennis and Robert Wood; Accomac by Dr. A. Watson and W. Dix; Northampton by W. P. Moore.

[34] Constitution, p. 11.

[35] Constitution, Article VI, clause 11.

[36] Article III.

provided in the law for white. The general assembly should make no law establishing slavery or recognizing property in human beings.[37]

Popular education was provided for in the new constitution, for the first time in the constitutional proceedings of Virginia. A poll-tax was levied on all male adults, one-half of which tax should be applied to free schools. The constitution declared that taxation should be equal and uniform throughout the State.[38]

Having made these great changes in the organic law, the convention adjourned on April 7, 1864. The constitution was then submitted to the people for ratification and was approved by about five hundred votes.[39] Apparently it is not known what vote was cast against it. The people seem to have had little affection for a government which derived its authority from military force. Under such circumstances, civil government soon came into conflict with the military supervision and was humiliated. In this way Mr. Peirpont's government came to grief in eastern Virginia in the summer of 1864. Norfolk was at that time under civil administration and paid taxes into the Alexandria treasury. But General Benjamin Franklin Butler, who was now in command in that district, did not like the civil establishment. He accordingly ordered an election on the question of abolishing it in favor of a purely military rule. Peirpont, in alarm, issued on June 22, 1864, an appeal "to the loyal people of Norfolk, Virginia," in which he gave notice of Butler's intention to hold the election, and protested strongly against it. Butler had his way, however, and announced the result in an order of June 30, 1864. The vote, he declared, was 330 to 16 against a continuance of civil government in Norfolk, "which gave as results to them only taxes and salaried officials without corresponding results."[40]

---

[37] Article IV, clause 21. [38] Article IV, clause 20.

[39] Alexandria Gazette, June 15, 1865. Statement of J. M. Botts.

[40] The order stated that only 108 votes had been cast at the former municipal election for all the candidates for the 45 offices in the city government.

All further attempts at setting up a civil administration in Norfolk were strictly forbidden.[41]

The Alexandria government was thus rudely shaken. Alexandria, Accomac, Northampton, Fairfax and Norfolk counties had been the real limits of its authority and now it lost its fairest provinces. In the last year of the war the area under Peirpont's administration shrank into the counties of Alexandria and Fairfax. No taxes were collected by the civil government in Norfolk and Portsmouth after June 24, 1864, and tax collections also ceased about the same time in Accomac and Northampton. In this shorn condition the Alexandria government lingered on until the end of the war.

The "Restored Government of Virginia" did not owe its existence to a popular demand for a Union administration in the eastern part of the State. It was founded for other purposes. It was in the first place the revolutionary government of West Virginia, when that section refused to follow old Virginia into the Confederacy. A short time afterwards the West Virginians decided to form a new State out of the northwestern counties. But constitutional limitation required that a State should give consent to the erection of a new State within its territory. It was here that the "Restored Government" was chiefly useful. For it was evident that Confederate Virginia would not consent to the establishment of a new Union commonwealth out of her ruins; the "Restored Government," however, might use the name of Virginia to secure the desired consummation. In this way the consent of Virginia was given to the separation of West Virginia and the Federal Constitution was satisfied. The same counties, whose representatives voted in the name of Virginia for the establishment of West Virginia, formed the latter State. This was merely

---

[41] Appleton's Annual Cyclopædia, 1864, p. 810. Peirpont complained bitterly of Butler's action in his message to the assembly in December, 1864.
Journal House of Delegates, 1864-5, p. 6.

the consent of West Virginia to her own establishment, and Virginia had no hand whatever in the matter.

The "Restored Government" would now have come to an end unless it was continued in the few counties of eastern Virginia which the Federals held. This course was decided upon. When Peirpont removed to Alexandria, the "Restored Government" consisted apparently of two men, the governor and Secretary of State Hagans.[42] The great majority of the population of the eastern counties were Confederates, but there were some slave-holders that adhered to the Union and a few Northerners resident in the section. This small minority formed the constituency and elected the little legislature.

The Alexandria government was not in itself of great importance. It governed but a few counties and under the shadow of bayonets; it was the rule of a few aliens in the midst of a generally hostile population. Men, at the time and since, have smiled at its legitimist pretenses. Yet it was recognized as the legal government of the State by the President of the United States. It is, however, as the forerunner of the reconstruction that the Peirpont government has its greatest interest. It formed a nucleus of the Republican party in old Virginia, and measures carried through by the Alexandria legislature, or proposed within it, were characteristic of the reconstruction. Thus the constitutional convention amended the constitution so as to abolish slavery, and did away with the laws that prescribed different punishments for whites and blacks. It was proposed to establish public schools, to repeal the laws forbidding negroes to be educated, and to give them the right to testify in courts, as well as other measures of the same liberal stamp. But there seems to have been no mention of negro suffrage, although it had been already thought of in the North. Many of the Republican leaders in the reconstruction period first became known by their participation in the Alexandria

[42] Wheeling Intelligencer, quoted by the Alexandria Gazette of May 14, 1863.

government. John C. Underwood, afterwards so well known as the Federal judge at Richmond, and the president of the constitutional convention of 1867-8, was elected a United States Senator by the Alexandria legislature. Peirpont became the provisional governor of Virginia during the reconstruction. John Hawxhurst was a widely-known Republican leader and a prominent member of the constitutional convention of 1867-8. Lewis McKenzie, who afterwards represented Virginia in Congress, was a Congressional candidate under the Alexandria government. S. Ferguson Beach was a well-known politician. James W. Hunnicutt, the most influential Republican leader in the early years of the reconstruction, attended a convention at Alexandria. Most of these men were not natives of Virginia. Peirpont came from West Virginia, but Underwood, Hawxhurst and Beach were Northerners. It will thus be seen that when Lee surrendered, a Union government existed in Virginia, whose members were afterwards to become Republican leaders, and radicals as well, as the Republican party grew in that direction.

## CHAPTER II.

### The President's Attempt at Restoration.

When Lee surrendered on April 9, 1865, and ended the war, the resources of Virginia had probably been more thoroughly drained than those of any other of the Confederate States. The country between the Potomac and Appomattox had been subjected to the repeated raids and continued occupation of the opposing armies, and farms were in a ruined condition, without farming implements and stock. In many cases crops had not been raised for years or had been repeatedly destroyed. But while industry lay in this prostrate condition, Virginia was more fortunate in a social and political sense than many of her neighbors. The private warfare which embittered Kentucky and Tennessee hardly existed at all in old Virginia, for her people were practically united in support of the Confederate cause. Furthermore the body of slaves freed from restraint by the emancipation did not outnumber the whites as in South Carolina or Mississippi.

But, of course, the future of the State depended very largely upon such a policy as the Federal government might adopt towards the conquered South. It seems clear that it was Lincoln's desire to re-admit the Southern States to participation in the Federal government as soon as they had abandoned all resistance to the United States. In the proclamation of December 8, 1863, (1) he offered amnesty to all but specified classes of leading men; (2) declared that a State government might be reconstructed as soon as one-tenth of the voters of 1860, qualified by State laws, "excluding all others," should take the prescribed oath; (3) declared that if such a government was republican in form, it should be benefited by the guarantee clause; (4) excepted

States where loyal governments had always been maintained; but (5) added that the admission of Congressmen rested entirely with the two houses, and not with the executive.[1]

In pursuance of this plan, State governments were established under Federal control in Tennessee, Louisiana and Arkansas before the war had ended. But Lincoln went further. One of the witnesses before the reconstruction committee testified that he offered the following terms to Judge Campbell, the Confederate commissioner at the Fortress Monroe conference:

(1) The disbandment of the Confederate armies.

(2) The full submission of the Southern people.

(3) The emancipation of the slaves.[2] This negotiation, however, with the Confederate government fell through.

Later the President went to Richmond, after the evacuation, and, it seems, offered to treat with separate States and to recognize the right of the Virginia legislature to recall its troops from the field. Judge Campbell replied that if the President would permit the legislature to meet, it would doubtless order the recall of the State troops. On April 6, 1865, Lincoln wrote to General Weitzel, in command at Richmond, directing him to permit the Virginia legislature to meet and withdraw the Virginia regiments from the Confederate army.

A few days later Lee surrendered; nevertheless the concilatory proceedings continued. The Richmond Whig of April 12, 1865, issued an address which requested the governor, lieutenant-governor, members of the legislature and other prominent citizens to assemble in Richmond on April 25. "The matters to be submitted to the legislature," it said, "are the restoration of peace to the State of Virginia, and the adjustment of questions involving life, liberty and

---

[1] Lalors' Cyclopædia of Political Science, etc., Vol. 3, p. 544. Messages and Papers of the Presidents, VI, 179.

[2] Appleton's Annual Cyclopædia 1865, p. 787. House Docs., Reports of Committees, 39th Congress, 1st session.

property." Safe conducts were issued for Robert M. T. Hunter, John B. Baldwin, John Letcher and other members of the former State government. The address was signed by a large number of prominent citizens and received the approval of General Weitzel. An informal meeting was held in Richmond on April 14, at which Judge Campbell recited the terms that the President offered. The assembly, thereupon, appointed a committee to inform Governor Smith and the legislature of the propositions. It seems, however, that Campbell exceeded his instructions, as President Lincoln, in a letter to Weitzel of April 12, 1865, declared that the former had misconstrued his order, and requested that his letter to the general and his paper to Campbell should be withdrawn.[3]

At all events, the assassination of Lincoln ended any such plan of re-adjustment. General Halleck took command in Richmond and refused to recognize the authority of the State officers. For some weeks government in Virginia remained in abeyance. In this interregnum, popular meetings were held at various places with a view to the re-establishment of civil government,[4] the most important of which was the one held at Staunton on May 8, 1865.[5] This meeting adopted resolutions declaring that the people of Augusta county were prepared to conform to the laws of the United States, and advised the assembling of a convention for the purpose of re-organizing the State government.

Virginia did not, however, remain long without civil administration. On May 9, 1865, President Johnson issued his proclamation, "to re-establish the authority of the United States and to execute the laws within the geographical limits known as the State of Virginia." This order declared the Confederate State and national governments null and void, and directed the appointment of revenue collectors, the re-establishment of postal routes, the holding

[3] Appleton's Annual Cyclopædia, 1865, 798.
[4] A. H. H. Stuart's "Restoration of Virginia to the Union," p. 12.
[5] "Restoration of Virginia," p. 12.

of the district court and provided for confiscation. The ninth article was the most important. It said, "That to carry into effect the guaranty by the Federal Constitution of a republican form of State government and offer the advantage and security of domestic laws as well as to complete the re-establishment of the authority and laws of the United States and the full and complete restoration of peace within the limits aforesaid, Francis H. Peirpont, Governor of the State of Virginia, will be aided by the Federal government, so far as may be necessary in the lawful measures which he may take for the extension and administration of the State government."[6]

The action of Johnson in recognizing the validity of the Alexandria government placed Virginia upon a different footing from that of the other States which had fallen with the Confederacy. Louisiana, Tennessee and Arkansas had come, before the end of the war, more or less under Federal control, and in these States governments had been already established by the Unionists. In the other Confederate States—North and South Carolina, Georgia, Florida, Alabama, Mississippi and Texas—the President appointed provisional governors. Constitutional conventions were held and governments re-formed.

But now that Johnson fully recognized the Alexandria administration, Virginia possessed a regular State government of her own. Two weeks later Peirpont went from Alexandria to Richmond, arriving there on May 26, 1865.[7] Soon after his inauguration, he issued a call for an extra session of the assembly. It met in Richmond on June 19, 1865. Three senators and nine members of the house of delegates were present. This was the last meeting of the Alexandria legislature.

The next day Peirpont sent in his message to the assembly. He treated the economic and political condition of the

[6] Messages and Papers of the Presidents, VI, 338.
[7] The Richmond Enquirer of April 2, 1868.

State with great fullness. He urged the necessity of the organization of county governments and the election of officers, and desired the legislature to pass acts legalizing the marital relations of negroes, increasing the assessment of taxes and increasing the legal rate of interest to 7¾ per cent. Furthermore Peirpont asked a most important concession of his legislature—the repeal of the disfranchising article of the Alexandria constitution of 1864.[8] In conformity with the governor's recommendation, the legislature passed acts staying the collection of debts and increasing the rate of taxation from ten to twenty cents on the hundred dollars' worth of property, and finally, on June 21, an act submitting to the popular vote at the next election the question of giving the assembly the power to alter and amend the third article of the Alexandria constitution, that which related to disfranchisement.

The brief session ended on June 23, 1865. Before adjournment, a resolution was passed declaring "That the general policy of the present Federal administration and especially its policy in regard to the reconstruction in Virginia, is eminently wise, just and proper and merits the warm approbation of the loyal people of Virginia."[9]

Speaker Downey finally congratulated the members that their action in the legislature had kept the State government out of the hands of the abolitionists. "Virginia," he said, "is now safe. Whatever they may do to other States, they cannot force a provisional governor upon her. Whatever they may do to other States, thank God, they cannot now saddle negro suffrage upon us."

This was a rather startling declaration, coming as it did from a member of the Alexandria government. But it must be remembered, besides the natural gratification of the little legislature in being recognized, that in June, 1865,

---

[8] "It is folly," he said, "to suppose that a State can be governed under a republican form of government when in a large portion of the State, nineteen-twentieths of the people are disfranchised and cannot hold office."

[9] Fredericksburg New Era, June 27, 1865.

no general sentiment in favor of negro suffrage existed. At this time some of the members of the Alexandria government seem to have been in sympathy with Governor Peirpont in his support of Johnson's policy of speedy reconciliation and restoration.

There was much work for Peirpont to do, in effecting the re-establishment of local government, which had well-nigh disappeared from the State in the ruin of war. For this purpose he appointed commissioners and conductors of county elections; in some cases the governor appointed these officers, in others he authorized any persons to act whom the military authority appointed.[10] Under these directions, and with the aid of the military, local government was speedily restored in most parts of the State.[11] There were some exceptions. In the municipal election in Richmond on July 25, 1865, ex-Confederate officers were elected mayor, commonwealth's attorney and superintendent of the almshouse.[12]

Shortly after the election, when the members of the board of aldermen met to organize the city government, an order was sent by General Turner declaring the election null and void. Accordingly there was no civil administration in Richmond until the following autumn. In October, General Terry allowed a quorum of the council to meet, in order to prepare for the coming election. The obnoxious officers finally resigned and the military authorities then permitted the organization of the government.

After this incident, Peirpont issued an order to the justices of the county courts, which forbade any persons to hold office who had participated in the Confederate government.[13] In this case Peirpont bowed to an obvious necessity; his own feelings were mild and conservative, but he

---

[10] Appleton's Annual Cyclopædia, 1865, p. 816. Fredericksburg New Era, June 27, 1865.
[11] Alexandria Gazette, August 29, 1865.
[12] Richmond Enquirer, October 30, 1865. Richmond Times, July 26, 1865. Richmond Republic, July 26, 1865.
[13] Fredericksburg New Era, August 4, 1865.

was forced to consider as paramount the authority of the general commanding in Virginia. It was, indeed, Peirpont's desire to carry out the mild Presidential policy and to reconcile Virginia to the North. This is evident not only in his message to the assembly and in his speeches, but in his whole course of action in the summer and fall of 1865. His appointments of judges were much commended by the conservative press. "He has secured for himself," said the Richmond Whig, "a hold on the good-will of the people of Virginia that neither the defamation of malice nor the intrigues of knavery can dislodge."[14] Peirpont constantly urged the necessity of such sacrifices as might placate the dominant section, and the avoidance of any possible occasion of irritation. Thus, in the important matter of the election of a president of the Richmond and Danville Railroad, he interfered, in order to prevent the chance of a misunderstanding. General Joseph E. Johnston was a nominee for the position, but Peirpont persuaded a majority of the stockholders that this election of the great Confederate field marshal would be untimely.[15] General Johnston was, therefore, defeated, receiving 1,728 votes to 2,288 cast for A. S. Buford.[16]

But Peirpont's policy, wise and conciliatory as it was, soon brought him into opposition to his former associates at Alexandria. For the majority of Union men in Virginia, who had supported the Alexandria government, were Republicans of radical tendencies. The strength of the radical party in comparison with the whole number of voters in the State was very insignificant. It consisted chiefly of farmers living in the counties along the Potomac, and of the tradesmen who had followed the Union army to Norfolk. Yet this faction, inconsiderable as it was, had hoped to control Virginia through the disfranchising article of the

---

[14] Alexandria Gazette, September 9 and 13, 1865.
[15] Fredericksburg New Era, October 3, 1865.
[16] Richmond Whig, September 14, 1865. Alexandria Gazette, September 15, 1865.

Alexandria constitution, which, if continued in force, would have disqualified for voting almost the entire population of the State. Accordingly, the action of the legislature, upon the governor's recommendation, in providing for the repeal of this section, surprised and angered the radicals. Lewis McKenzie said in his testimony before the reconstruction committee: "When that legislature went to Richmond (June 19, 1865) they altered the constitutional provisions in such a manner that I found that the loyal men of the State were to be totally sacrificed and turned over to the power of the secessionists." [17]

The opposition to Peirpont's policy took form even before the June meeting of the legislature. On June 12, 1865, the Republicans of Alexandria formed a political association with S. Ferguson Beach as president. The following resolutions were adopted: (1) "That it was essential to prevent Virginia from coming into the control of the secessionists; (2) that it seemed as if this control might be gained; (3) that the constitution of Virginia should be amended so as to confer the right of suffrage upon, and restrict it to, loyal male citizens without regard to color." [18] This "Union Association of Alexandria" further issued an address to the people of the North requesting Congress to regard the administration of Governor Peirpont as merely provisional, and to order an election of members to a State convention, in which "loyal people" without distinction of color should vote. Congress was also requested to organize a territorial or provisional government until the meeting of the convention.[19]

This was the first announcement of the advocacy of negro suffrage by the Republican party in Virginia. But unqualified negro suffrage was not proposed at this time. It will be further noted that Governor Peirpont's former associates in the Alexandria administration now desired the overthrow of the very government which they had

---

[17] Reports of Committee, 39th Congress, 1st session, Part 2, p. 11.
[18] Alexandria Gazette, June 13, 1865. [19] Ibid., July 5, 1867.

supported and maintained to be legal during the Civil War, and upon whose legality rested West Virginia's claims to Statehood. The Alexandria Republicans took this remarkable position because they feared that the administration was passing beyond their control. They thought that Peirpont had abandoned them. And indeed he had ceased to be the governor of a single town and had become, in a large sense, the governor of Virginia.

The Alexandria address was a fair sample of radical sentiment. A meeting of the "Unconditional Union men of Frederick county" was held at Winchester on June 28, 1865, "for the purpose of giving expression to their opinions upon the recent action of the Virginia legislature in extending the right of suffrage to rebels and their aiders and abettors."[20] The radical farmers adopted resolutions expressive of astonishment and dissatisfaction at the course of Governor Peirpont, the legislature and Speaker Downey. A memorial was also addressed to President Johnson condemning the removal of restrictions upon disloyal voters and asking such legislation as would prevent "rebel officeholders" and "aiders and abettors of rebellion" from holding office. It is evident from these and similar expressions that the radicals in Virginia strongly opposed the plan of speedy reconciliation. They opposed not only the re-enfranchising of Confederates, although this was a prime grievance which threatened their political fortunes, but chiefly the restoration of government with the entire exclusion from suffrage of the colored race.

In the same measure that the President's policy toward the conquered States surprised and alarmed the radicals, it surprised and cheered the conservative population of Virginia. At first Johnson's intentions were not entirely clear. The thirteenth clause of the amnesty proclamation, which excluded from pardon all ex-Confederates possessed of more than $20,000 worth of property, was felt to be an

[20] Alexandria Gazette, July 8, 1865. Richmond Republic, July, 1865. Fredericksburg New Era, July 18, 1865.

anomaly and a hardship. A meeting in Richmond sent a memorial to the President declaring that this exception had acted in a ruinous manner upon the interests of all classes. Judge John C. Underwood made the most of the clause, and, under his directions, John Underwood, United States marshal of Eastern Virginia, libelled much property for confiscation.[21] Little came of this action, however, as Johnson opposed a confiscation policy, and, after a time, abandoned the thought of it entirely.

It soon became evident that he wished to restore the Confederate States to their old place in the Union as speedily as possible, and with this assurance the hopes of the Southern people began to rise. The President sanctioned the election of members of the legislature, and also of Congress, in anticipation of a return of representatives from the South to Congress. Accordingly, numerous candidates appeared in every district. For the most part they were self-nominated and stood solely on their own merits. No organized parties existed in Virginia, except the Republican, which had a partial organization in a few localities but on the whole was small and uninfluential. The great body of voters, former Democrats and Whigs, had now no very settled political principles. But to some extent the future development of politics was apparent. Distinctions between the old parties had largely passed away, and where they lingered, lingered chiefly as memories. There were indeed few party divisions, except in the border counties, which had been invaded by Northern settlers. The latter brought radical ideas with them and stood for a new order of things founded on the victory of the Union arms. But the great majority of the people were conservatives and held to the ancient political beliefs, especially to that of the essential difference between the races.

Political interests had begun to revive in the State as people recovered from the first shock of the overthrow of

[21] Alexandria Gazette, June 11 and 17, 1865. Richmond Bulletin, June, 1865. Alexandria Gazette, July 17-18, 1865.

the Confederacy. The tone of the press soon became independent, sometimes imprudent and even bitter. Accordingly several newspapers were suppressed by the military authorities. The Richmond Whig received notice to suspend publication on July 11, 1865, by order of General Turner, for an attack on President Johnson.[22] The Whig was again issued on July 26, and thereafter stood as a champion of conciliation. The Petersburg News was suppressed in June, 1865, the Richmond Bulletin in October,[23] the Richmond Examiner, the Richmond Times and other papers at various times. But in spite of occasional outbreaks, a part of the press favored adaptation to the new circumstances, and there seemed in 1865 a general desire on the part of the Virginia people for reconciliation with the North. The war was now a little past and the bitterness of reconstruction had not come. In August, 1865, the Richmond Whig urged Virginia and all the Southern States to adopt the thirteenth amendment at once;[24] and the Richmond Times joined with the Whig in calling for an extra session of the legislature, in order that the North might appreciate the fact that the State was loyal. Meetings of citizens were held in various towns to testify to the loyalty of the Virginia people to the Federal government.[25] The one in Richmond on August 29, 1865, passed resolutions denouncing "the persistent and wicked efforts of a portion of the press and people of the Northern States to brand the people of the South with perfidy and insincerity . . . by questioning their fidelity and truth in the oaths of allegiance which they have taken."[26] Furthermore the course of President Johnson and Governor Peirpont was approved.[27]

As the time for the election approached, numerous candidates for the legislature and for Congress appeared. It

---

[22] Alexandria Gazette, July 16, 1865. [23] Ibid., October 9, 1865.
[24] Richmond Whig, August, 1865. Alexandria Gazette, August 18, 1865.
[25] Alexandria Gazette, August 26, 1865; also August 18, 1865.
[26] Richmond Whig, August 30, 1865. Alexandria Gazette, August 31, 1865. [27] Alexandria Gazette, September 13, 1865.

was a time of personal politics, for there was no great difference between most of the candidates. The newspapers were full of cards announcing the qualifications of various aspirants, who chiefly differed in their ability or inability to take the Congressional test-oath. The fortunate candidate who possessed this advantage published it as a prime reason for receiving support. Real party contests took place in only a few counties which contained a radical element.

The Congressional and State elections were held on October 12, 1865. The vote was exceedingly small, amounting to only 40,000 in the eight Congressional districts. No Republican was elected to Congress. In the Alexandria district, where the largest radical vote was cast, Lewis McKenzie received 1,722 votes, and his conservative opponent 4,853.[28] The poll in this district was 8,670 less than in 1860. Several of the Congressmen elected could not take the test-oath, among them the distinguished Alexander H. H. Stuart.

Power was granted to the legislature to enact the proposed amendment to the Alexandria constitution by an almost unanimous voice. In 59 counties only 772 adverse votes were cast. Many counties voted unanimously for it, and in several no vote at all was taken on the question. The election was thoroughly representative of the desires of the people. By the terms of the act of legislature, little restriction was put upon the voters beyond taking the amnesty oath. Consequently the Congressmen and nearly all of the members of the legislature were conservatives.

It was a question now in what manner the Congressmen-elect would be received by Congress. Would they be required to take the test-oath? Many denounced such a procedure as unconstitutional, but the Richmond Whig, while

---

[28] Alexandria Gazette, November 17, 1865. Reports of Committees, 39th Congress, 1st session, Vol. 2, p. 159. One hundred and fifty other votes were scattered.

it denied the constitutionality of the oath, argued that it would be impossible to gain representation without it.[29]

According to President Johnson's plan, the restoration should now have ended. Armed resistance had long ceased in the Southern States; they were apparently reconciled to their enforced return to the Union; they were apparently loyal to the Federal government. Representatives had been elected to Congress. All that remained to be done was the acceptance of the new Congressmen by that body, and peace would return again to the stricken States.

But great struggles cannot be so easily composed. The victors do not so readily relinquish their advantages. Besides, the chief issue of the great war remained unsettled. The North was absorbingly interested in the new status of the manumitted race. Slaves they were no longer; but should they still remain under the control of the white race, without political rights? President Johnson, who was a Southerner and had supported the Northern side rather from loyalty to the Union than from any desire to liberate the blacks, was content that they should remain in their present condition. Not so with the Congressional majority. The act of emancipation remained incomplete in its eyes, for the freedmen had not been raised to citizenship; the reconstruction, therefore, was yet to begin. And when the two powers of government came to oppose each other, it was found that the Northern people would lend support to the legislature against the executive.

Upon the meeting of Congress in December, 1865, the representatives elected by Virginia and the other Southern States went to Washington with hopes of being admitted to their seats. But they were disappointed. The clerk of

---

[29] "It is no use," it said, "for us to be guilty of the folly of butting our heads against immovable walls. We must take things as we find them and we must accept facts as they are and devote all our thoughts and energies to the single end of getting back under the protection of the Constitution and laws of the United States."—Whig, October, 1865.

the House, McPherson, omitted the names of the Southern members from the roll-call, and they were not permitted to plead in their behalf.[30] All that was left for them was to return home. In such manner Johnson's attempt at restoration failed.

---

[30] A. H. H. Stuart's "Restoration of Virginia to the Union," p. 16.

## CHAPTER III.

### The Beginning of the Reconstruction.

When Congress on December 4, 1865, refused to receive the Southern representatives, it was evident that harder terms would be required of the late seceding States. The period of the President's supremacy, from May to December, 1865, had passed. Afterwards came a year of inquiry and of discussion on the part of the Congressional majority, and then the reconstruction. In Virginia the reconstruction proper was comparatively brief, lasting from March 2, 1867, to January 28, 1870, a period much shorter than was experienced in South Carolina, Louisiana and Florida, where it continued for quite a decade.

For some time after the downfall of the Confederacy, the policy of the Republican party towards the Southern States remained uncertain. As the year 1865 wore on, the party lost confidence in Johnson and then became rapidly hostile to his policy. The President's hasty attempt to renew the Federal relations of the Confederate States was partially responsible for this hostility, and to this was added the conduct of these States themselves. The emancipation had suddenly thrust forth upon the South an immense, homeless, laboring population, which, in its new-found liberty, was not inclined to settle down immediately to industry. Such a condition of affairs was alarming and possibly dangerous. The Southern legislatures attempted to correct it by passing codes that were, in some cases, restrictive to the point of rigidness.[1] The North had been narrowly watching the course of the Southerners in regard to the negroes and the new codes at once stirred up an exceedingly

---

[1] Wilson's "Division and Reunion," p. 260.

active and bitter criticism. It is true that Virginia had had no share in these legislative proceedings when Congress met on December 4, 1865, but her legislature speedily adopted vagrant laws which placed her in the same class, in the Northern opinion, with the other Confederate States.

The new assembly, which passed the vagrant acts, met on December 4, 1865. It was a representative body and accordingly conservative. Some members, indeed, had served under the Confederate government. John B. Baldwin, of Augusta, one of the ablest politicians in the State and a former member of the Confederate Congress, was elected speaker of the house of delegates. But none of the prominent leaders in the secession movement, such as Robert M. T. Hunter and William Smith, were present. The National Intelligencer said of this body: "It is a curious fact that in the house of delegates, ninety-six, or with one exception, every member is an old time Whig, while in the senate it is pretty much the same."[2]

The assembly at once showed its representative sentiment. The restrictions imposed on Confederates as to suffrage were removed on December 8, 1865, when, in accordance with the result of the recent election, the disfranchising article of the Alexandria constitution was repealed.[3] The legislature substituted no other conditions for voting and made no further reference to disfranchisement. It next attempted to bring about a reconciliation with West Virginia. The war had shaken and well-nigh wrecked the State, but this, the first legislative body of the new era, went immediately to work to regain for Virginia all that was yet possible. On February 15, 1866, the assembly passed an act appealing to West Virginia to reunite with Virginia and directing the appointment of a committee to negotiate with West Virginia concerning the payment of her share of the State debt.[4]

The all-important problem that confronted the assembly

---

[2] Fredericksburg News, December 7, 1865.
[3] Acts, 1865-6, p. 197.
[4] Acts, 1865-6.

was the proper method of legislation in regard to the manumitted blacks. The freedmen had not yet become satisfactory workers under the new conditions. They showed a tendency to break contracts at will, and many of them roamed the country without restraint. In order to regulate this idle population and to obtain labor, which was sorely needed, the legislature passed a vagrant act.[5]

Vagrants were to be hired out for terms not exceeding three months; the wages they earned should be applied for their benefit with some restrictions. If a vagrant ran away without sufficient cause, the person hiring him might have his services free for one month in addition to the stipulated term of labor, and might work him with ball and chain. If the employer refused to take him back, the vagrant could be used in the public service or hired out for his keep. In the case of his not being needed for any of these purposes, he might be confined in jail on bread and water.

This law was probably justified by the economic necessities of the time, since there was an urgent demand for labor in many sections and a large part of the freedmen refused to work for the small wages possible. Besides a great many negroes had become nomads. But the passage of such an act was most impolitic in view of the temper of the Northern people at that period. Although the Virginia vagrant law was milder than those of other Southern States, at the same time it gave great offense. It seemed to savor of slavery. In the heat of the moment many thought that Virginia sought to nullify the emancipation. This was the view of the military commander. On January 25, 1866, General Terry issued an order stating that "The ultimate effect of the statute will be to reduce the freedmen to a condition of

---

[5] Acts, 1865-6, p. 91. Vagrants were: (1) All persons who unlawfully returned to counties or towns whence they had been legally removed. (2) Persons without means who refused to work for common wages. (3) Persons refusing to perform the work allotted to them by the overseers of the poor. (4) Beggars, unless disabled or incapable of labor. (5) Persons from without the State who did not work and had no visible means of support.

servitude worse than that from which they have been emancipated—a condition which will be slavery in all but its name. It is therefore ordered that no magistrate, civil officer or other person shall in any way or manner, apply or attempt to apply the provisions of said statute to any colored person in this department."[6] General Terry further charged that the law was passed in the interest of the landholders, who had combined to put down wages; and when the negroes refused to take what was offered, wished to compel them to work.

It is true that there had been attempts in some sections to arrange a scale of wages, but this seems to have been due rather to the impoverishment of the farmers than from a desire to oppress the negroes. It has been urged that this combined arrangement of wages tended to protect the freedmen, as no farmer might offer them less than the prescribed rate[7] and then force them to work. The legislators seem to have wished to act fairly and Terry's order was exaggerated. But unquestionably in many cases the law would have worked harshly. The chief error, however, lay, not in any great wrongfulness of the statute, but in the very effort to enforce a restrictive measure in the face of Northern feeling, for the members of the legislature could not have been ignorant of that sentiment. Immediately upon the publication of General Terry's somewhat rhetorical order, the anti-Southern press was filled with attacks upon the law, which did great injury to Virginia. Probably nothing that was done by the Southern people in the reconstruction so irritated the North as the passage of various laws for the regulation of freedmen.[8]

---

[6] Fredericksburg News, January 26, 1866. New York Tribune, January 29, 1866. Lalors' Cyclopædia of Political Science, III, 547.

[7] It was apparently five dollars a month and board.

[8] New York Evening Post, May 30, 1866: "In South Carolina and Florida the freedmen are forbidden to wear or keep arms. In South Carolina they are forbidden to work at trades, or to engage in business, unless specially licensed. In Florida it is made a penal offense to teach the freedmen or their children, except a license has first been obtained. In Mississippi all freedmen who are not engaged in

On the other hand, acts were passed for the benefit of the blacks. The legislature, on February 26, 1866, legalized the marital relations of negroes in cases of cohabitation, and made legitimate the children of such connections.[9] The Freedmen's Bureau report in 1866 mentioned the great benefits effected by this enactment.[10]

Further, in order to protect the freedmen in their ignorant condition, the law declared that no contract should be binding for longer than two months unless signed and acknowledged before a justice of the peace, notary public, or other officer of the law, or before two credible witnesses. It was also required that the meaning of the contracts should be explained to the negroes. Most of the distinctions in law between the races were abolished. All provisions in respect to crimes and punishments were applied equally to both. Legal phraseology was changed so as to do away with discriminations. Georgia and South Carolina had adopted elaborate codes for the regulation of freedmen, but the Virginia legislators decided against such a course.[11] The acts relating to slaves and slavery were repealed on February 27, 1866. The right of testifying in courts in cases which concerned them was granted the freedmen, and the right of bearing testimony in all cases might have been extended but for the strong prejudice of the white people on that point, especially of the lower classes.[12] Unfortunately the vagrant act neutralized the effect of this wise legislation in the eyes of the North. Furthermore, the

---

labor by the year are compelled to take out a license. . . . In South Carolina it is enacted that the laborer shall be called 'servant' and the employer 'master.' North Carolina, Georgia, Alabama and Tennessee appear to be liberal and in the main just."

[9] Acts, 1865-6, p. 85.

[10] Senate Docs., 39th Congress, 2nd session, Vol. 1, p. 157.

[11] Testimony of W. T. Joynes before the reconstruction committee. Reports of Committees, 39th Congress, 1st session, Part 2, p. 160.

[12] Testimony of W. T. Joynes before the reconstruction committee. Reports of Committees, 39th Congress, 1st session, Part 2, p. 16, and Report of Secretary of War, 39th Congress, 2nd session, p. 717.

assembly irritated the Virginia Republicans by electing new State officers in place of those who had come from Alexandria with Governor Peirpont.[13]

The vagrant acts and negro codes passed by the Southern States unquestionably added greatly to the already bitter hostility of the Congressional majority. They were one of the causes of the reconstruction. The inquiry of the reconstruction committee, which began early in 1866, supplied another incentive to rigorous measures against the South. This inquiry gave the Southern radicals an opportunity to bring forward their grievances and opinions at a very critical time. The Republican witnesses testified almost unanimously to the unfitness of the late Confederate States for re-admission to their constitutional rights; and they made a deep impression upon Congress. The Unionists in the South expected the war to bring about an impossible reversal of conditions and opinions; they naturally resented the prevailing prejudice against them, and they wished to rule the country.

In the case of Virginia the investigation began on January 23, 1866. Forty-nine witnesses were examined.[14] The majority were prominent Republicans. They spoke as men entirely discontented with the community in which they lived, and their testimony agreed in being adverse to the loyalty of Virginia, although it differed somewhat in details. Some witnesses were much more moderate in their estimates of the faults of the Virginia people than others. But they mainly agreed that the Virginians were still hostile to the Federal government and actually disloyal; that Union men were hated and that their lives would be endangered if the United States troops should be withdrawn; also that the freedmen were frequently ill-treated and that they and white Unionists could not hope for justice in the State courts. A few witnesses even asserted their belief that in

---

[13] Alexandria Gazette, January 12, 1866.

[14] Reports of Committees, 39th Congress, 1st session, Part 2, Virginia. Reports of Secretary of War, 39th Congress, 2nd session.

case of a foreign war the former Confederates would join the enemy against the Union. The chief adverse witnesses were General John W. Turner, in command at Richmond; Judge John C. Underwood; Lewis McKenzie, lawyer; Dr. G. F. Watson, direct tax commissioner; John Hawxhurst; George Tucker, lawyer; Josiah Millard, assessor of internal revenue; Jonathan Roberts, sheriff of Fairfax county; Dr. J. J. Henshaw; John F. Lewis, farmer; Colonel Orlando Brown, commissioner of the Freedmen's Bureau; Major-General A. H. Terry, and Charles H. Lewis, secretary of the commonwealth. Nearly all of these men, and most of the other Republican witnesses as well, had come originally from Northern States. The leading witnesses who attested to the good intentions of the Virginia people were W. T. Joynes and General Robert E. Lee. General Lee's evidence was particularly important. He expressed his belief in the entire loyalty of the people to the United States government and in their desire to do justice to the freedmen. Joynes testified to the loyalty and well-meaning of the Virginia legislature. However, the favorable impression of the few conservative witnesses was overborne by the far greater number of Republicans,[15] and the majority report of the committee affirmed the unfitness of the Southern States for self-government and re-admission to their Federal relations.

The testimony of the radicals played, therefore, an important part in occasioning the reconstruction in Virginia. They had, indeed, opposed the new State government from the first, when it became evident that Peirpont had decided upon a conciliatory policy. The refusal of Congress to receive the Southern members greatly encouraged them. A meeting of Republicans was held at Alexandria on Feb-

[15] Reports of Committees. Some testimony was absurd. For instance, George S. Smith was asked, "If left to themselves what would they (Virginia people) do with the negro?"

Answer. "They would entirely extirpate him from the face of the earth. They would first commence with the Union men and then they would take the negroes."—p. 14.

ruary 5, 1866, with Judge Underwood presiding.[16] The resolutions called upon Congress to establish a territorial government, for the protection of "loyal" men, as the existing State government was unsafe.[17] The inquiry of the reconstruction committee followed by its report strongly adverse to the South; and the passage of the Freedmen's Bureau bill .and civil rights bill increased the radical activities. An attempt was made at party organization at the "Unconditional Union Convention" meeting at Alexandria on May 17, 1866.[18] It elected John Minor Botts president. Botts was born in Dumfries, Virginia, in 1802. He became a prominent Whig politician and served several terms in Congress. Later he refused to acquiesce in the secession, took no part in the war and suffered imprisonment for a time by the Confederate authorities.[19] The Republican party in Virginia was particularly fortunate in having such an able and influential man for a leader, but it did not avail itself of the advantage, as the negroes considered Botts too conservative.

Sixty delegates were present in this convention, representing seventeen counties. Credentials, however, were reported from only nine, and many delegates came without authorization. On May 18, the convention formed an organization under the title of the "Union Republican Party of Virginia." It defined the policy of the party concerning the negro for the first time.[20] The resolutions urged disfranchisement of Confederates and a qualified suffrage applying to both races. This declaration in favor of negro suffrage was not reached without considerable debate, for some delegates considered the resolution to be inexpedient.[21] This convention marks the first regular organization of the Republican party in Virginia. Hitherto organization had been

---

[16] Alexandria Gazette, February 6, 1866.
[17] Ibid., February 17, 1866.
[18] Alexandria Gazette, May 18, 1866, and Enquirer of same date.
[19] Appleton's Cyclopædia of American Biography.
[20] Alexandria Gazette, May 19, 1866, and New York Tribune of same date.
[21] New York Tribune, May 19, 1866.

confined to localities; it now included the State. The platform adopted called for negro suffrage, but with restrictions to be determined by law. Indeed Botts and his followers continued to oppose "manhood suffrage," until it became evident that the national Republican party had adopted it as its policy.

While the Republicans were thus building up a party, the conservatives did not remain entirely idle. The chief political event of the summer of 1866 was the attempted union of Northern and Southern men in a new party, to uphold President Johnson in his policy of restoration. No parties existed in Virginia at the time, except the Republican party. Accordingly it was necessary to revert to old machinery, to elect delegates from Virginia to the conservative convention at Philadelphia. A called meeting of the executive committees of the Breckinridge, Bell and Douglas parties of 1860 was held in Richmond on July 16, in order to consider the propriety of appointing delegates to this convention.[22] Some few members of the ante-bellum committees met and resolved to recommend the election of delegates and in accordance with the recommendation these were appointed from the Congressional districts. The convention assembled in Philadelphia on August 14, 1866.[23] The meeting was largely attended and enthusiastic. Men from the North and from the South fraternized and adopted conciliatory resolutions. The conference was not without result; it tended somewhat towards bringing about a better feeling between the sections and in favor of Johnson. But the advantage proved to be entirely temporary and failed to arrest the movement towards radicalism.

The conservative convention gave rise to a similar demonstration from the radicals. They therefore met in Philadelphia on September 2, 1866, for the purpose, as it was announced, of bringing Southern Unionists into touch with

[22] Richmond Enquirer, July 17, 1866.

[23] New York Tribune and Richmond Enquirer, August 15; also Lalors' Cyclopædia of Political Science, Vol. 3.

Northern Republicans.[24] Many prominent leaders from both sections attended. The delegates, of whom there were a great number, divided into two conventions, Northern and Southern, and considered the burning question of the hour —negro suffrage. The members from the far Southern States favored universal suffrage, while the views of the border States remained uncertain, many of their delegates being adverse to it. The Northerners opposed an unlimited extension of the franchise, as they feared the effect of a radical declaration on the fall elections. John Minor Botts, the leader of the Virginia delegation, contended strongly against the grant of unlimited suffrage, but his fellow-delegates from Virginia refused to support his attitude.[25] James W. Hunnicutt offered a resolution declaring that the enfranchisement of all men with the exception of "rebels" was the only safeguard of Virginia and the nation, and George Tucker brought forward a similar motion. The convention lingered on for some days, debating the all-engrossing subject. Finally the committee on suffrage went over to the extreme radical position and brought in a report in favor of "manhood" suffrage, which was adopted by the very small vote of 66 to 8.[26] Many delegates had left Philadelphia. After this convention the Republican party adopted as its policy the extension of the privilege of voting to all men without regard to limitations.

The year 1866 was one of growing excitement and bitterness. The Southern people had hoped for speedy restoration to the Union upon the Presidential plan. When, however, Congress thwarted Johnson's purpose and passed the Freedmen's Bureau bill and the civil rights bill, hope gave way to indignation and dismay. The press no longer

---

[24] New York Tribune, September 3, 1866. The Virginia delegation was the largest from the Southern States, numbering 61. Texas sent 15 delegates; Louisiana, 18; West Virginia, 51; Alabama, 4; Kentucky, 13; Mississippi, 30; Arkansas, 2; North Carolina, 7; Maryland, 60; Delaware, 6; Florida, 7; District of Columbia, 27.

[25] New York Tribune, September 6, 1866.

[26] Ibid., September 10, 1866.

urged conciliation of the North,[27] but passive resistance.[28] Racial antagonism began to be felt, for the negroes inclined to assert themselves in their joy over the Congressional measures. In Norfolk, on April 16, 1866, the freedmen held a procession in celebration of the passage of the civil rights bill. Many of them bore arms. The parade turned into a riot, in which two whites and two negroes were killed. The city was put under martial law and an investigation ordered. It seemed that both sides were at fault.[29] Except for a few such disturbances, however, the conduct of the blacks was still generally orderly. But there was a feeling of unrest, uncertainty and bitterness in Virginia and throughout the South at the hostile attitude of Congress; while in the North, criticism of the South was unsparing. Two incidents in Virginia in 1866 increased the hostility of the Northerners towards her. The first was a decision of Judge Thomas at Alexandria adverse to the civil rights bill.[30] One of the parties to a case in court brought forward colored witnesses, but Judge Thomas decided that the laws of Virginia forbade negro testimony in cases where only white men were parties, and that Congressional law could not impair the rights of the State to decide the competency of witnesses. The other incident was more serious. Doctor J. L. Watson killed a negro in Rockbridge county on November 13, 1866.[31] He was tried by a State court and acquitted. On December 4, Watson was arrested by command of General Schofield and ordered to be tried before a military commission acting under the authority of the act of Congress of July 16, 1866. When the commissioners assembled

---

[27] Enquirer, May 1, 1866: "We can advise no more humiliations. It is idle for us to pay price after price for what they have never had a right to withhold, but which they have the power and will to deny, after the price is paid, the same as before."

[28] Enquirer, June 26, 1866.

[29] Executive Docs., 39th Congress, 2nd session, No. 72, and Enquirer, April 17, 1866.

[30] Alexandria Gazette, May 25, 1866. Fredericksburg News, May 29, 1866. Appleton's Annual Cyclopædia, 1866, p. 765.

[31] Senate Docs., 39th Congress, 2nd session, Vol. 2, No. 29, p. 17.

on December 19, a write of habeas corpus, issued by the circuit court of Richmond, was served them, but General Schofield refused to surrender the prisoner. However, by the advice of the United States Attorney-General, President Johnson discharged the commissioners and released Watson.[32] This case produced an unfortunate impression upon the North.

It was in these gloomy times, on December 2, 1866, that the legislature met for its second session. The governor's message advised measures of conciliation and submission,[33] and the advice was wise. It urged a modification of the vagrant act, a revision of the road laws and the laws regulating county taxes, and, most important of all, the ratification of the fourteenth amendment. But the legislature and the people of Virginia could not bring themselves to accept it. The press flared up in opposition. The assembly decisively rejected the amendment on January 9, 1867, by a vote of 27 to 0 in the senate and of 74 to 1 in the house of delegates.[34] This action was a mistake, as later events proved. Virginia found herself compelled to accept the fourteenth amendment in the end. At the same time it was natural that the legislature should reject it while there was yet any hope of escape.

The regular session of the Virginia assembly closed on March 3, 1867. Very important measures, however, were pending in Congress, and the legislature on March 1 adopted a joint resolution requesting Governor Peirpont to call an extra session immediately, in order to take steps to meet the emergency. Peirpont complied, and on March 4 sent in his message,[35] which communicated the terms of the reconstruction act passed by Congress on March 2, 1867.

---

[32] Appleton's Annual Cyclopædia, 1866, p. 765. Richmond Enquirer, December 18-19, 1866.
[33] Journal House of Delegates, 1866-7. Enquirer, December 4, 1866. Enquirer, January 10, 1867.
[34] Enquirer, January 10, 1867.
[35] Journal House of Delegates, 1866-7. Richmond Enquirer and Whig, March 5, 1867.

The message was sadly reminiscent, regretted that the governor's former advice to ratify the fourteenth amendment had been rejected, and advised the legislature to accept the new law and make provision for calling a constitutional convention.

The advisability of holding such a convention to frame a new constitution in accordance with the requirements of Congress was then brought up in the assembly. The temper of the members had altered since their former sweeping rejection of the fourteenth amendment, and they were in the mood to accept the governor's advice, which events had proven wise. A bill, providing for the holding of a constitutional convention at Richmond in the same month, was presented in the senate and passed by a vote of 25 to 4. No vote was taken on it in the house of delegates. Probably the house would also have accepted the measure, but the supplementary reconstruction bill of March 23, 1867, rendered the further action of the legislature in the matter useless. That body continued in session for some time, and on April 20, 1867, passed an act which gave the freedmen the right to testify in the State courts in all cases. This conciliatory measure, however, came too late for any benefit.

The reconstruction act of March 2, 1867, changed the State of Virginia into Military District Number One. General John M. Schofield, who had hitherto been military commander of the State, was now made commander of the district. He assumed control on March 13, 1867. On that day he issued an order informing the people of the act of Congress, and declaring that he would supercede the civil authorities only so far as it was necessary in the discharge of his duties. "The undersigned," he said, "appeals to the people of Virginia and especially to magistrates and officers, to render the necessity for the exercise of this power as slight as possible by strict obedience to the laws and by impartial administration of justice to all classes." [36]

[36] Richmond Enquirer, March 14, 1867.

In this fashion the reconstruction began in Virginia. It was brought about by many causes, but the chief cause lay in the democratic theories which had been so long agitated in the North. For the reconstruction, as the term is known in American history, was the attempt of the majority in Congress to compel the Southern States to recognize the civil and political equality of the colored race. Such a program, in States where the two races were nearly equal in numbers, would necessarily produce the most novel and perplexing social and political phenomena.

## CHAPTER IV.

### The Freedmen's Bureau and the Union League.

The acts of March 2 and 23, 1867, which admitted the freedmen to suffrage, gave rise to one of the most remarkable political contests in history. The mere grant of the ballot to the negroes, however, did not necessitate a break in the relations between masters and men. At first, indeed, it was a question whether the traditional influence of planters over slaves would not continue to prevail, and the colored vote be largely under conservative control. In the early months of 1867 many Southern people hoped for such a result.[1] John Minor Botts, a politician of long experience, declared his opposition to negro suffrage, because he believed that the freedmen would support the Democratic policies. As the white men in the South had not been able to resist the influences of that party, how could the negroes?[2]

This illusion was quickly dispelled. Doubtless if the freedmen had been left to themselves by their Northern friends, they would have united with their former masters and have voted solidly at their dictation. The negroes would hardly have been able to assert their independence of the white race without outside assistance. But new forces had begun to work upon them. The Union soldiery, the schools taught by radicals, Northern settlers, itinerant politicians—all moved the blacks to sever their old connections. But potent as such agencies were, some strong form of organization was necessary to bring about that solid array of the black race against the white which was a feature of the reconstruction. This result came largely through the Freedmen's Bureau and the Union League. By means of the

---

[1] New York Tribune, March 17, 1867.
[2] Richmond Enquirer, July 8, 1867.

former institution the control of the negroes was taken out of the hands of the planters and given over to Northern officials. The bureau thus existed in the community as a foreign and independent judicial, social, economic and political power. Consequently, by the spring of 1867, it had done much to emancipate the colored race from Southern dominance. But it might have been expected that the blacks would be outgeneraled politically by the astute whites. Yet this did not happen. On the other hand, the freedmen were well organized and incorporated as a body in the Republican party. The radical politicians accomplished this clever feat by means of a political secret society called the Union League.

At the close of the Civil War, the freedmen found themselves confronted by the responsibilities as well as the privileges of freedmen. They were not well prepared for the sudden manumission, and they naturally wished to enjoy this novel liberty. Some of them indeed remained on plantations, but thousands wandered about idly, committing many depredations, or else hastened to the cities and towns.[3] Consequently there was a great scarcity of farm laborers, and agriculture suffered.[4] The farmers could not afford to pay good wages and the negroes were unwilling generally to work for little. Moreover, emancipation had unsettled their minds by promising a new future. It was proper, therefore, that the Federal government, which was responsible for emancipation, should have made some provision for the immediate care of the homeless, propertyless race.

The characteristic institution of the reconstruction, the Freedmen's Bureau, was established in Virginia on June 15, 1865, when the assistant commissioner, Brevet Brigadier-General Orlando Brown, took charge of the freedmen's

[3] Richmond Whig, July 10, 1865. Ex. Docs., 1st session, 39th Congress, No. 72, p. 144.

[4] Alexandria Gazette, August 2, 1865. Fredericksburg New Era, July 6, 1865.

affairs in Richmond. The State was now divided into eight districts, with an assistant quartermaster as the superintendent of each; and the districts were in turn divided into sub-districts under the command of military officers.[5]

The directions of the superintendents instructed them to protect the negroes in their rights as freemen; to see that they were not oppressed; to cultivate friendly relations between the two races; to assist in the organization of schools; to discourage the tendency of the negroes to idle roaming; to urge upon them the importance of making labor contracts; to furnish rations, medicine and medical attention; in a word, to establish a paternal supervision of the colored race. Courts were also established by the bureau to decide all cases concerning negroes in which the penalties did not exceed three months' imprisonment or the fine of a hundred dollars. The whites and negroes were invited to select one representative for each race to assist in conducting this court.

As soon as the Freedmen's Bureau was established the government handed over to it large tracts of land that had been libelled for confiscation or seized upon the ground of abandonment.[6] These amounted in all to 96,752 acres. This land was applied to the benefit of the freedmen in various ways; some of it was worked by them on shares; some was cultivated by the government, the freedmen being paid wages; in other cases farms were rented by the blacks or let to them free of charge. By the decision of the President these lands were gradually restored to the owners,[7] so that 40,751 acres had been returned by November 31, 1865. By October 27, 1866, the bureau held only 10,182½ acres, most of which was woodland.

The bureau also supported a great number of negroes on rations. In August, 1865, 178,120 rations were issued to

---

[5] Senate Documents, 39th Congress, 1st session, No. 27, p. 144, and House Executive Docs., 1st session, 39th Congress, No. 70.

[6] Appleton's Annual Cyclopædia, 1865, p. 375.

[7] Senate Documents, 39th Congress, 1st session, No. 27, p. 145, and Senate Documents, 39th Congress, 2nd session, Vol. 1, No. 6, p. 157.

15,779 people; in September, 275,880 rations to 16,298 people; in October, 235,786 rations to 11,622 people. By September, 1866, however, the number of persons fed by governmental charity had fallen to 4,679.[8] Some of the supplies were given to destitute whites as well as to negroes.

Schools for the freedmen were established at military posts by various benevolent societies[9] with the active aid and coöperation of the Freedmen's Bureau. The Shenandoah Valley was largely furnished with teachers by the Baptist Association. By November 31, 1865, there existed 90 schools with 195 teachers and 11,500 pupils.[10]

One of the most important functions of the bureau was the regulation of labor contracts for the freedmen. A great general impoverishment oppressed the State and the wages offered, therefore, were necessarily low. In some sections the farmers tended to combine to fix the wage rate.[11] This coöperation acted to the disadvantage of the freedmen, and by General Order No. 8 of the district of the Nottaway, issued on June 22, 1865, public meetings for the purpose of arranging a scale of wages were prohibited. But such combinations among the farmers continued to be one of the alleged grievances of the freedmen for some time. It is easy to understand, however, how difficult it would be for the employers to adjust themselves both to hard times and to new labor conditions.

In every way of life the Freedmen's Bureau affected and influenced the colored population.[12] In some respects it was

---

[8] Only 2,869 were fed by November 1, 1867. Report of Secretary of War, 40th Congress, 2nd Session, Vol. 1, p. 240.

[9] An important one was the American Tract Society.

[10] By March 31, 1867, there were 228 teachers and 15,340 pupils. 25,000 colored children received some instruction.

[11] Senate Docs., 39th Congress, 1st session, No. 27, p. 144. It is said that the rate was fixed at five dollars with rations.

[12] The special correspondent of the Nation in 1865 gives a vivid description of the bureau courts: "In one corner of the empty court-room the sergeant had set up his desk. . . . A good many people came in—now it was an old farmer who entered; now it was a negro, hat in hand, with a question or a grievance or a request for transportation; now it was a citizen who came in to hear what decision had been made in reference to the case of a friend, or to vouch for the friend's good character."—The Nation, 1865, p. 268.

a useful and beneficent institution. But, however much good the bureau may have done the negro, it was thoroughly disliked by the white people. It was an alien control of the working population; it intervened between the planter and the laborer, between white and black. It oftentimes saved the freedmen from injustice. It oftentimes gave ear to causeless and silly complaints on the part of the negroes, who were, of course, prone to use its power of protection to the utmost.[13]

The work of the Freedmen's Bureau may be generally classified under four heads: (1) Benevolent. The negroes were given food, clothing, medicine and other necessities, farming implements and even brief land tenures in some places. (2) Protective. The freedmen received protection, both within their courts and without, from any aggression on the part of the whites. The bureau agents also supervised the making of all labor contracts. (3) Educational. Schools were established under the jurisdiction of the bureau. (4) Political. The agents naturally possessed a very great influence over their wards, which was usually exerted in the radical interests. This last activity became important after the negroes were granted suffrage in 1867.

The bureau generally obtained a strong hold on the blacks, for its benefits were positive and its functions many-sided, concerning every phase of life. But it could not exist as a permanent institution and partially relinquished authority over the freedmen to the civil officials. The bureau courts were closed on May 10, 1866, and the whole jurisdiction resigned to the State courts, in order that the operation of these courts might be tested while there was opportunity for observation by the bureau agents. The latter were required to be present at trials of freedmen to see that they received justice. The agents reported that in some sections partiality existed on the part of the courts towards the whites. In criminal cases the blacks were given

---

[13] "Why the Solid South," p. 238.

justice in the main, although with many exceptions. As the magistrates of Elizabeth City, York and Nansemond counties refused to perform their work, the bureau courts were reopened in those counties in July, 1866. The bureau reports stated that the freedmen were willing to work for fair wages. The agents usually drew up contracts for them. The rate of wages was about nine dollars a month and rations, an advance over that of the year 1865. The negroes, like the whites, paid taxes per capita, all males above sixteen years of age being subject to taxation.[14]

Concerning the benefit of the Freedmen's Bureau to the community and to the freedmen, there was an absolute conflict of statements. The reports of the agents naturally represented it as a very beneficial institution. Most of the Virginia Republicans, too, supported it; they declared that it protected the freedmen in their rights. On the other hand, the greater part of the white people of Virginia cordially detested it. They represented it as fomenting strife between the races and as supporting a large number of negroes in entire idleness, and, in fact, the management was open to considerable criticism.

It appears that when first instituted the bureau was a benevolent aid society. The freedmen, unaccustomed to responsibility, required some such friendly tutelage. It was then a benefit. But it also seems clear that the bureau degenerated greatly in its last stages, in the attempt to discharge political functions. It then generally became a disturbing instead of a harmonizing influence in the community. But the institution was peculiar and arose out of the needs of the time. Its character depended largely upon the character of the individual agents, for each one exercised a more or less independent authority. In some districts, where men of integrity and sense conducted the affairs of the blacks, the bureau was useful. In other districts, which were managed by incompetent and unworthy

[14] Executive Docs., 39th Congress, 2nd session, vol. 1, No. 6, p. 157.

agents, the institution was a positive evil, and unfortunately this was very often the case. It is a question whether the Freedmen's Bureau was justified in interfering in politics to the large extent that it did; at any rate, the interference was unfortunate, and yet circumstances probably made it inevitable, for the prime function of the bureau consisted in furthering the independence of the colored race.

The Freedmen's Bureau awakened some criticism in the North. Thus, Generals Steedman and Fullerton, sent from Washington to observe conditions in the Southern States, brought back a report decidedly adverse to the bureau. According to this report, its general effect was to awaken antagonism between the races. The agents exercised a wide legal jurisdiction, trying cases involving real estate titles, crimes and even divorce. Their decisions were by no means invariably just.[15]

The negroes were naturally loyal to the Freedmen's Bureau. It did much for them; in one sense, it liberated them, yet there were a few colored critics. Willis A. Hodges, in a speech before the Virginia constitutional convention on January 3, 1868, declared that abuses were practiced upon the freedmen in certain cases by agents. He stated that provisions and clothing intended for negroes were appropriated by some agents and that the blacks working upon government farms received no pay and suffered from actual privations.[16] But Hodges was not sustained in his charges by his fellow Republicans in the convention. They, in general, thoroughly approved of the Freedmen's Bureau.

The peculiar political institution of the reconstruction was the Union League. This Republican society was formed at the close of the Civil War. It soon included the chief towns in the North, and in 1867, with the extension of suffrage to the negroes, entered the ex-Confederate States. The society had a national organization and local branches;

---

[15] Richmond Enquirer, May 16, 1866.
[16] Debates of the Convention, p. 163.

and deputies were sent from the different States to the central council.[17] "The league was organized as an aid to the effective carrying out of the humane objects and purposes of those in the North who believed that the ballot in the hands of the negro would be preferable to bullets in the muskets of a standing army, which would have been necessary for an indefinite period in many sections of the South."[18] The Union League was a secret society, to which few but negroes and the white leaders had access. The club always met at night and the chief exercises consisted in the political education of the freedmen. "It was a system of night school in which they were instructed in the privileges of citizenship and the duties they owed to the party which had made them free and given them exercise of suffrage."[19] The services were conducted in total darkness. The members formed a circle inclosing the candidates for admission and moved around with shuffling gait, while from the corner of the room came the lugubrious sound of clanking chains.[20] Lights were then brought in and the blacks received further instruction as to their political duties.[21] The great strength of this secret society system lay in the fact that the white radicals could teach their doctrines to the freedmen without the counteracting effects of contradiction and argument, which they must have met if they had attempted to conduct their campaign solely from the stump. Besides the negroes were bound to a uniform course of action by oaths and by the example of a closely organized association.[22] Consequently the Union League exerted an immense influence over the colored race. This became evident in the election of 1867, when the conservative whites, in spite of all their efforts and the ties of old association, were able to influence only 638 blacks

---

[17] Letter of General Edgar Allen in the author's possession. General Allen was the grand deputy for Virginia.

[18] Letter of General Allen.

[19] Letter of General Allen.

[20] Ibid. The negroes often came fifteen or twenty miles to attend these meetings.

[21] Enquirer, November, 13, 1867.

[22] Enquirer, October 31, 1867.

to vote against the convention out of a total colored vote of 93,145.

The power of the Union League differed considerably in the various States. The League had a masterly organization in Virginia and held the blacks well in hand for several years. In Louisiana it seems not to have been so strong; at least it did not occupy as conspicuous a place in the public attention as in some other States.[23] In South Carolina the League was particularly powerful. The Klu Klux Klan directed its attacks against it. According to the testimony of Governor Robert K. Scott, in the contest case of Hoge vs. Reed, Republicans who were killed were usually leaders of the Union League.[24] The graduated system of league government placed a great power in the hands of a few white men. Thus a witness in the contest case of Reed vs. Simpson, the secretary of the Union League, was also a deputy, which gave him the supervision of the eight clubs in Anderson county, South Carolina.[25] Consequently the Klu Klux Klan, in striking at the carpet-bagger leaders, undermined the whole system of negro supremacy; and the outrages it perpetrated had much to do in the destruction of the league in certain States. In other States the decadence of the institution was effected by more peaceful means. In Virginia many planters adopted the plan of discharging laborers who were members of the Union League. A still more potent cause of destruction was the schism in the Republican party in 1869, whereby the unity of the league was seriously disturbed. It seems to have gone to pieces after 1870.[26] While the lifetime of the League was thus

---

[23] Ms. Docs., 41st, 42nd Congress.

[24] House Ms. Docs., 1st session, 41st Congress, Hoge vs. Reed, p. 42. A witness testified that one B. F. Randolph organized the Union League in South Carolina, for which offense he was killed. Hoge vs. Reed, p. 34.

[25] House Misc. Docs., 1st session, 41st Congress, Reed vs. Simpson, p. 53.

[26] Contested Elections, 1875-6, 1st session, 44th Congress, Platt vs. Goode. The League apparently was not in existence in Virginia in 1875.

short, its activities were very great and its influence appeared to threaten the supremacy of the white race. The society was singularly adapted to the character of the freedmen, and the men who organized and managed it were often acute and masterful politicians. The Union League threatened to place the negro race in permanent power in several States; consequently the whites made it the point of attack, and when they succeeded in breaking it down, they had mastered one of the chief issues in the contest for supremacy. The effect of the Union League in Virginia was to completely separate, politically, the black race from the white.

## CHAPTER V.

### THE STATE CAMPAIGN OF 1867.

The Freedmen's Bureau had prepared the freedmen for independent political action, when, in March, 1867, the acts of Congress conferred upon them the privilege of suffrage. Even before the bureau had well advanced in its activities, the negroes of the northern counties, excited by contact with Republican settlers, organized the first political movement of their race in Virginia. A convention assembled at Alexandria on August 2, 1865, with fifty delegates present from various counties, and adopted resolutions appealing for the extension of suffrage to the colored race.[1] This movement, however, proved abortive. But it was significant of the growing radical spirit. The Republicans of Virginia had come, as we have seen, to favor negro suffrage by the summer of 1865. After the Philadelphia radical convention of 1866, they abandoned all idea of restricting the franchise by property or educational qualifications or military service; and unitedly advocated "manhood suffrage" for the colored race. Congress, by the reconstruction acts of March, 1867, granted the blacks the privilege of voting for members of the constitutional convention of the Southern States.

Immediately, migrating politicians from the North and the Virginia Republicans began to organize the negroes by means of the secret society known as the Union League. The Freedmen's Bureau had made the colored race independent of the whites; the Union League now thoroughly drilled it in practical politics and so prepared for a Republican victory at the polls. The firm establishment of negro suffrage

---

[1] Alexandria Gazette, August 3, 1865, and Fredericksburg New Era, August 18, 1865.

in Virginia was the leading feature of the radical policy. Other benefits for the freedmen were also desired. Some extremists advocated confiscation of Confederate property in favor of the negroes. The majority of Republicans, indeed, did not favor such a severe measure, but the blacks, ignorant and naturally desirous of bettering their condition, seized upon the idea with great avidity. It soon became the dream of the freedmen to own their farms instead of working for wages. They believed that the Federal government intended to divide lands among them, to give each head of a family "forty acres and a mule."[2] The freedmen were partly justified in this hope by the attitude of the extreme radical wing of the Republican party under the leadership of Thaddeus Stevens, and by the consequent talk of the soldiers, bureau agents and others.[3] The rumor of an intended distribution of land by governmental agency had grown widespread and produced further disturbances in the labor system, for the negroes in many cases refused to sign contracts, hoping to possess lands which they might work themselves.[4] But it became evident in 1867 that Congress would not follow Stevens in his proscriptive policy, and the Republican leaders in Virginia discouraged the hopes of the blacks as to confiscation. Yet the latter did not abandon them for a considerable length of time. The radical policy comprehended a constitutional assurance of colored suffrage, the opening of public offices to negroes, and, in general, the gain of political and civil equality for the freedmen. So eager were the blacks to vote that three days after the passage of the reconstruction act of March 2 they attempted to participate in a municipal election at Alexandria.[5] For the first time, negro suffrage became an

---

[2] This familiar phrase probably originated in a speech of Thaddeus Stevens delivered at Lancaster in September, 1865. Lalor's Cyclopædia of Political Science, etc., III, 544.

[3] Appleton's Annual Cyclopædia, 1865, p. 375.

[4] Alexandria Gazette, October 4, 1865.

[5] Richmond Enquirer, March 8, 1867, and Alexandria Gazette, March 6, 1867.

immediate and practical question. Governor Peirpont asserted that the colored men were undoubtedly entitled to vote under the terms of the reconstruction act. Mayor Latham and Judge Moore consulted President Johnson and the United States Attorney-General upon the right of freedmen to participate in the election, but received no definite answer.[6] In this uncertain state of affairs the commissioners of elections decided to refuse negro voters. When the polls were opened the blacks came forward to present their votes, which were declined by the commissioners but recorded by a committee appointed for that purpose in the radical interest. About 1,400 votes were cast by the negroes; more than 1,000 by the conservatives, and only 72 by the white radicals.[7] This election occasioned considerable hostile comment in the North. Senator Wilson proposed in Congress that it should be annulled, because the votes of the negroes had been refused. The occurrence of similar incidents was prevented by an order from General Schofield, prohibiting all local elections while registration was in progress.[8]

Immediately after the publication of the act of March 23, 1867, arrangements were made for registration under that law, and a board was appointed by General Schofield to select suitable persons as officers of registration.[9] In making these selections preference was given to officers of the army and of the Freedmen's Bureau; secondly, soldiers honorably discharged were chosen, and lastly, Union citizens. On April 2, 1867, an order was issued by Schofield suspending all elections under the provisional government until the registration should be completed. Vacancies which might occur were to be filled by temporary appointments of the commanding general.[10]

---

[6] Richmond Enquirer, March 8, 1867.
[7] New York Tribune, March 8, 1867.
[8] Appleton's Annual Cyclopædia, 1867, p. 758. Order of April 2, 1867. Ex. Docs., 2nd session, 40th Congress, No. 342.
[9] Appleton's Annual Cyclopædia, 1867, p. 758.
[10] Appleton's Annual Cyclopædia, 1867, p. 758, and Ex. Docs., 2nd session, 40th Congress, No. 342.

The summer of 1867 was a very busy one in Virginia politics. The organization of the radical party went steadily on throughout the State. No better method than the Union League could have been chosen for uniting the negro race with the Republican party, for through the secret society the radical propaganda might be carried on, largely without fear of interruption on the part of the native whites. In these clubs the raw masses of freedmen were politically instructed and transformed into a powerful machine; few of them were able to withstand the pressure brought to bear and remain without the fold.[11] Naturally the Union Leagues,[12] as they were called,[13] soon became a subject of bitter and repeated attacks from the conservative press.

But protest and abuse were quite fruitless, and the radical agitators penetrated to every county of the State, addressing the freedmen and inspiring them with alluring hopes.[14] The most prominent politician of this time was James W. Hunnicutt. He was a clergyman, a native of South Carolina, but had lived for many years in Fredericksburg, where he published a religious newspaper. Hunnicutt had been a slave-holder and voted for the ordinance of secession, although by his own statement, unwillingly. Later he became a Union man and in the beginning of the reconstruction went actively into politics as an advanced radical. His utterances were sometimes violent and even dangerous. Both as a speaker and as editor of the leading Republican journal in Virginia, the Richmond New Nation, he exerted a very great influence over the freedmen. In the Philadelphia convention Hunnicutt had withstood the more conservative views of John Minor Botts upon negro suffrage. He now became the chief leader in the radical ranks.[15]

---

[11] Enquirer, September 5, 1867. [12] Enquirer, September 6, 1867.

[13] They were known as "Loyal Legions" and by several other names, but "Union League" was the one most used.

[14] Enquirer, June 13, 1867, and September 6, 1867. Fredericksburg News, September 18, 1867.

[15] New York Tribune, April 12, 1867, and Enquirer, April 20, 1867.

The Republican State Central Committee, composed of Lysander Hall, John Hawxhurst, Burnham Wardwell, W. R. Smith, James H. Clements and Lewis McKenzie, issued, on March 20, 1867, an invitation for a State convention. This convention assembled at Richmond on April 17, 1867.[16] Two hundred and ten delegates were present, of whom 160 were negroes. Forty-nine counties were represented. The convention was entirely under the influence of Hunnicutt and his supporters and was accordingly radical. The freedmen took a very prominent part in the proceedings and made many of the speeches, which were sometimes inflammatory. Confiscation was demanded by the negroes, almost to a man;[17] they went much farther than their white leaders in urging and approving this measure. The committee on resolutions provided the following series: First, Congress was thanked for the reconstruction act, the beneficial effects of which were felt in the increased security of "loyal" men. Secondly, the principles of the Republican party were adopted as a platform, and the coöperation of all the classes, without distinction of race or color, was invited. The third resolution proclaimed equal protection to all men before the courts and equal political rights, including the right to hold office; free schools for all classes, and a free and equal participation therein; a more equitable system of taxation, which should be apportioned on property only; and a modification of the usury laws, to induce capital to flow into the State. The fourth resolution declared that all men are free, equal, etc., and pledged the party to a strict adherence to these sentiments. Fifth, the party was bound to support no man for office who did not openly identify himself with it and support its principles. The sixth resolution recognized the interests of all the laboring classes of the State as identical, and denied the wish to deprive any white laborer of his privileges.[18]

---

[16] Enquirer and Whig, April 18, 1867.
[17] New York Tribune, May 17, 1867.
[18] Richmond Enquirer, April 19, 1867.

Hunnicutt's first attempt at party direction had proven a success. He controlled the workings of the April convention. The greater part of the negroes were completely under his influence. But there remained a considerable element of opposition within the Republican ranks, composed of men of less extreme views and led by John Minor Botts. He had been beaten by Hunnicutt in the contest for leadership, but he still hoped to be able to found a party that might obtain the support of both white and black, a party that would secure the rights of colored men, but which would not be dominated by the political and social ideals of radicalism. Unquestionably such a party would have been acceptable to many intelligent people in the North, who viewed with disfavor the clamors of turbulent negro factions under the control of agitators.[19] Some of the leading Northern newspapers commented severely upon the extravagance of the radical propaganda in Virginia. The New York Tribune advised the negroes to follow Botts rather than Hunnicutt. But the former had lost his prestige for the moment and Hunnicutt held the reins of power.

At this time there were two efforts made to form the Republican party in Virginia upon different lines from those advocated by Hunnicutt.[20] One of these movements was within the State; the other originated in Washington. It was clearly seen in the capital that the extreme measures of the Hunnicutt faction would necessarily tend to drive the white people into an antagonistic party to the lasting disadvantage of Republicanism. Accordingly an attempt was made to supercede Hunnicutt as a leader and to build up a party of more moderate views, of white as well as of

---

[19] New York Tribune, April 12, 1867: "To organize a campaign on the Hunnicutt plan is to abandon any hope of a permanent Union party in the South. We cannot afford to array the white against the black or the black against the white."

New York Times: "He (Hunnicutt) and such as he are unceasing in their endeavors to organize the blacks as a party that shall hereafter control Southern affairs and with this view they teach the superiority of the negroes as a race over the white."

[20] Enquirer, May 1 and May 7, 1867. Whig, May 1, 1867.

black supporters. Senator Wilson of Massachusetts came to Virginia, to lend his influence to the furthering of this plan. He made speeches in a number of towns, appealing to the blacks and also seeking to gain the adherence of white votes.[21]

Senator Wilson's mission, although it failed to draw the freedmen from their radical leaders, had an effect upon the political situation.[22] It somewhat strengthened a second effort to form a Republican party which was already under consideration among a part of the Virginia people opposed to Hunnicutt. They thought that Virginia could never regain her rights of Statehood unless under the Republican party, and that the best way of attaining the desired consummation lay through the frank acceptance of negro suffrage and the other demands of the North. Consequently a party should be organized for the purpose of conciliating the Congressional majority and thereby winning restoration. The Richmond Whig became the leading organ of the new movement, partly perhaps from its traditional hostility to the Democratic party. The key-note of the Whig's advocacy was the uselessness of resistance, the necessity of submission.[23] The Whig advised the Virginians to unite in

---

[21] New York Tribune, April 25, 1867. Enquirer, April 23, 1867. In Richmond he said that "He wanted the colored men who had been elevated from chattelhood to manhood. . . . He wanted the men who had been reluctantly dragged into the rebellion, who were impoverished by it, but who had no sympathy with it and the men who were deluded into secession but who had abandoned, amid the fire, blood, and desolation of war, that wicked heresy and who honestly complied with the demands of the country—he wanted all these classes to unitedly stand together on the national platform of the Union Republican party. . . . He appealed to the old Whigs of Virginia . . . to seize the occasion, unite their fortunes with the Union Republican party of the country and put down the secessionists."

[22] The Enquirer, April 20, 1867.

[23] Whig, April 5, 1867. "It is known," it said, "that the respectable Union men are bitterly opposed to Hunnicuttism in all its phases, and will not coöperate with the faction that is swayed by it. . . . What we all have to do is to save Virginia—her character and her fortunes. Unless we do so she will fall a prey to creatures more foul than the obscene birds of mythology. There are three classes that must unite to do so. . . . These three classes we have already in-

such a party and not to attempt any alliance with the Democratic party of the North, which, it declared, was utterly unable to benefit the South.[24] An especial appeal was made to the old-time Whigs, to assist in this effort for the restoration of the State.

A meeting in the interest of the new movement was held in Petersburg at the last of April. The Republican party, as it then existed in the State, had no share in the conference. An organization was not attempted, but a platform was adopted which was intended to be conciliatory to the North.[25]

The Petersburg platform, however, was the expression of only a few and attracted few supporters. It was too radical for the majority of the Virginia people and was condemned by the press.[26] The Whig still continued to urge the necessity of holding public meetings all over the State for the purpose of ratifying the following resolutions: "(1) We yield an unreserved submission to the requirements of

---

dicated—the better class of Union men like Governor Pierpont, Mr. Stearns . . . those who upheld the Southern cause, and the better class of colored population."

[24] Whig, April 22, 1867: "This party (Republican) can, for it has the power, give us self-government and admit us into the Union, and as we have said, it is under a pledge to do so. . . . The Democratic party would, we believe, do the same, if it had the power, but it has not. As our object is restoration, we propose to pursue that policy which will most effectually accomplish it, without regard to party antecedents or political creeds. We shall feel in doing this that we are best serving Virginia."

[25] Richmond Whig, May 1, 1867. It resolved "(1) That we agree to accept and perform in good faith the terms and conditions prescribed by the Congress of the United States as the terms and conditons upon which Congress has agreed to restore Virginia to her place in the Union. (2) That we recognize and accept as an essential part of said terms and conditions the proposition that the political power of the State, which has heretofore been wielded by white men alone, shall henceforth be possessed and exercised by white and black alike. (3) That we will therefore insist that a new constitution shall be framed for Virginia which shall provide that all men, white or black, without reference to previous condition of servitude, shall be perfectly equal before the laws, both in respect to political privileges and power and of civil rights; and that all laws creating distinctions or differences of any sort between persons of different races shall be unconstitutional, null and void."

[26] New York Tribune, May 17, 1867.

Congress. (2) We adopt the assurance and pledges of the Petersburg platform. (3) We will support Unionists for office like Governor Peirpont and Mr. Stearns." But the pleading of the Whig was without effect and the attempt to form a white conservative Republican party failed entirely. For a moment the movement seemed to die out; evidently without the coöperation of the other Republican elements in the State, it would be fruitless.

Meanwhile the radical propaganda was being actively carried on and the temper of the freedmen had grown more aggressive. In the latter part of April there were disturbances occasioned by the attempts of the negroes to ride in street cars with the whites. In the end they gained the right. On May 11, Zedekiah Hayward, an agitator, was arrested, charged with inciting the negroes "to acts of violence, insurrection and war."[27] He had urged the blacks to assert their right to ride in street cars, to sit in churches and theaters, to attend any schools and to enjoy any rights which the white people of Massachusetts possessed. Riots broke out in Richmond, on May 11-12, 1867, in which the freedmen seem to have been the aggressors; it was necessary to employ troops to restore order.[28]

Opposition still existed in the Republican party to the extreme views of James Hunnicutt and his followers. Botts had been disconcerted by his success in drawing the negroes over to the extreme radical position, but he had never abandoned the hope of building up a party under his own control. The supporters of the Petersburg platform accepted his leadership, as it was evident that they could form no organization of their own, and once more gave him a following. Botts had never considered the work of the April convention to be legitimate. He and his followers, among whom were Governor Peirpont and L. H. Chandler, objected to the authority by which it had been called. They complained that it represented comparatively few counties

---

[27] New York Tribune, May 20, 1867. Richmond Enquirer, April 27, 1867, and May 13, 1867.

[28] Enquirer, May 13, 1867.

and was composed largely of negroes, "and they declared that the Union citizens of Virginia would not come into a party imperfectly organized and exclusively led."[29]

Accordingly a call was issued for a new convention, to be held at Charlottesville on July 4, for the purpose of organizing the Republican party in the State.[30] It was signed by more than 300 men, some of whom were Virginians of property and rank, mostly former Whigs. That branch of the party led by Hunnicutt and the platform of the April convention were completely ignored.

The situation threatened a break in the Republican ranks into conservative and radical factions. The reconstruction committee now interfered to preserve peace. It gave over to the Union League Clubs of New York, Philadelphia and Boston the task of composing a quarrel "that threatened to disturb the harmony and unity of the party, not only in Virginia but throughout the South." The differing State leaders and the Northern mediators came together in Richmond, at the governor's house, on June 16, 1867. Some fifty men were present, among them Governor Peirpont, Judge Underwood, Senator Wilson, John Jay of New York, General Strong, John M. Botts, J. W. Hunnicutt, John Hawxhurst, L. H. Chandler and other prominent politicians.[31] Speeches were made by the leaders on both sides. Hunnicutt and the other radicals defended the validity of the April convention and refused to take any part in the proposed Charlottesville conference.[32] It was finally decided to abandon the Charlottesville meeting, and to hold another State convention at Richmond on August 1, for the purpose of drawing up a party platform. Botts was forced to accept the compromise. The result of the meeting was decidedly in Hunnicutt's favor.[33] It appeared evident from the action of their leaders that the mass of freedmen still remained under his influence; and while the question

---

[29] New York Tribune, June 15, 1867.
[30] Enquirer, May 21, 1867. [31] New York Tribune, June 15, 1867.
[32] Enquirer, June 19, 1867. [33] New York Herald, June 17, 1867.

of party organization remained open, the new convention was to be held in Richmond, the center of radical influence.[34]

But Mr. Botts still had hopes of winning the Republican leadership and of bringing the black men to a more moderate position, which would enable the native whites to join with them in a party.[35] Indeed, the political advent of the negro was too recent for his ideas to have become crystallized, and the antagonism of the races had not reached its later pitch of hatred. Therefore the advocates of conservative Republicanism made considerable progress through the months of June and July, 1867. Many men were anxious to end the reconstruction and felt that it was useless to oppose negro suffrage. They were so desirous of a speedy reconciliation that they were willing to make compromises to gain that end. The hopeless struggle against fate had better be abandoned. "What is the Republican party?" asked the Richmond Whig. "It represents and wields the whole power of the government. It is to all intents and purposes the government. To oppose it is to oppose the government."[36]

The movement for coalition between the native white people and the blacks suddenly came into prominence in July. It was chiefly the result of the efforts of the Richmond Whig and was noteworthy for the men who supported it; they were former Confederates and many of them exerted a local influence.[37] A large number of the citizens of Albemarle county met at Charlottesville on July 1, to consider the question of "coöperation." Thomas Wood was elected chairman and Captain John L. Cockran, secretary. The committee on resolutions consisted of Colonel John J. Bocock, Wm. T. Early, William Brand, W. F. Gordon, R. G. Crank, W. H. Southall, John Wood, Jr., W. E. Garth, G. B. Brown, J. W. Mason, J. R. Barksdale, John H. Bibb, Colonel R. T. W. Duke, Dr. J. R. Baylor, J. S.

[34] Enquirer, June 19, 1867.
[35] New York Herald.
[36] Whig, June 6, 1867, again June 25, 1867, and June 24.
[37] Whig, June 2, 1867.

Coles, A. J. Farish, Edmond Coles, Dr. A. G. Dulaney, B. R. Eddins, J. H. Simms, Colonel R. W. Wyatt, Dr. J. W. Michie, J. W. Chewning, Dr. W. C. N. Randolph.[38]

The chairman explained that it was the object of the meeting to determine the wisest course to take to secure the speedy reconstruction of the State upon the best possible terms. The resolutions declared "That having consented in good faith to the reconstruction of the Southern States under the Sherman-Shellabarger bill, we consider ourselves as bound in honor to the unconditional maintenance of the Union of these States, and that we regard the welfare of Virginia and of the other Southern States as requiring that our people should coöperate with the party that will give us protection for life and property, and believing that the Republican party of the United States alone has the power to give us protection, we desire to coöperate with them."[39] Forty-six delegates, most of whom were the aforementioned members of the committee on resolutions, were appointed to represent the "coöperators" in the August convention of the Republican party.

This was the fairest offer that party had ever received in Virginia. For these men exerted a social influence which had been hitherto lacking in it. The movement threatened a breach in the unity of the white race. The "coöperation" convention at Charlottesville was followed by others in Louisa,[40] Charlotte,[41] Amelia, Pittsylvania,[42] Smythe, Halifax,[43] Buckingham,[44] Rappahannock, Prince Edward and perhaps in other counties. In Charlotte, W. T. Scott, Dr. P. H. Flourney, William Cardwell, J. N. Edmunds, Dr. J. D. Spraggins, Colonel H. A. Carrington, Glasgow McGraw, Silas Mack, W. H. Smith, J. H. Holmes, Miller Davenport and Edward Nelson were elected as delegates; in Halifax, Hon. T. S. Flournoy, T. S. Green, J. B. Stovall,

---

[38] Whig, July 3, 1867.
[39] Enquirer, July 2; Whig, July 2.
[40] Whig, July 9, 1867.
[41] Whig, July 23, 1867.
[42] Whig, July 25, 1867.
[43] Whig, August 1, 1867.
[44] Enquirer, July 6, 1867.

M. P. Ensey, M. L. Booth, A. L. Meeks, together with several negroes.

By the end of July the coöperation movement had grown into considerable prominence. It was upheld by moderate men, who were prepared to abandon the Confederate tradition for the sake of Virginia's interests. The "coöperators" accepted negro suffrage because it was a fact. They wished to draw the freedmen to their support[45] and to lead them in a party, which should advocate in a general and conservative way the measures of reconstruction. Naturally the leaders would have been white men. The negroes were not offered confiscation, social equality, high office and other inducements. Their place, most likely, in such a party would have been a lowly one and their direct power small. But, on the other hand, their right to vote would have probably been established.

But the negroes were in no mood to play a subordinate part. The age was full of dreams; they were beginning to believe that boundless opportunities of advancement opened before them; and men who held the present hope of race equality would not rest satisfied with the advantages already gained. One of the most prominent negro politicians, Lewis Lindsay, in a characteristic and bitter speech at Charlottesville on July 2, announced the desires of the black men. He demanded a fair division of all offices. He claimed the right to social equality, and stated that the negroes intended to elect the governor, the members of Congress and a portion of the legislature. Wherever twelve men were appointed for any purpose, six of them must be black.[46]

Not only was the coöperation movement too conservative for the negroes; it could not have been otherwise than fatal to the influence of Hunnicutt and his fellow radicals. For their power lay in the impossible hopes with which they inspired the freedmen; no place would be open for them in a

---

[45] Whig, July 5, 1867. [46] Charlottesville Chronicle, July 2, 1867.

party led by moderate men of conservative aims. Consequently radicals, white and black, did not favor coöperation.[47] With Hunnicutt in this position, it was likely that the coming convention would be a final trial of strength between him and Botts for the control of the colored race; and the event would probably have a decisive effect upon party positions in the State.

On July 31, the day preceding the meeting of the Republican convention, Botts held a caucus of the conservative members, submitting a platform for their approval. It declared that secession was treason and that treason was crime, advocated free speech without license, and the payment of the public debt, except the Confederate. It also called for the enfranchisement of all concerned in the Confederacy but the leaders. The latter should be punished.[48]

The convention met at Richmond on August 1, 1867. The freedmen were alive with eagerness. They assembled at the African church, where the convention was to sit, as early as seven o'clock in the morning, and when the doors were opened at eleven, poured in and took complete possession. Two thousand negroes were left outside the church, together with Mr. Botts and the "coöperator" delegates, who had come to take part in the proceedings. No attempt was made by the radical leaders to reduce the mob to order. Many of the country negro delegates were also excluded. It was proposed to hold a meeting in the Capitol Square and the crowd outside went off there. Mr. Hunnicutt addressed the "mass convention" within the church, which consisted entirely of negroes except the fifty white delegates to the April convention. He said that all that was necessary for the present convention to do was to endorse the April platform. If any man did not feel disposed to vote for that declaration, he might go home and take care of his family. Those who supported the April platform should do the work of the August convention.[49]

---

[47] New Nation, July 4, 1867 quoted by the Enquirer of July 6, 1867.
[48] Fredericksburg News, August 2, 1867.
[49] Enquirer, August 2, 1867.

Meanwhile the crowd, which had been unable to gain admission to the church, assembled in the Capitol Square. John Hawxhurst was elected chairman. "Amid much confusion, the white coöperators, who had been excluded from the African church and kept out in the blazing sun while the darkies were inside, were again pressed to the outskirts of the meeting like the white fringe on the edge of a black blanket."[50] A proposition to invite Botts to speak was solidly voted down, and the platform of the April convention adopted.

The next day the convention met with reduced members. A colored delegate, Dr. Bayne, moved for an immediate adjournment, although Hunnicutt was in favor of a longer session. He wished the convention, he said, "to wind up like a Georgia camp-meeting—with a general jollification." He then defined his position. He favored the disfranchisement of all rebels; they should be excluded from suffrage until they were willing to work in any gear that might be put upon them. Notwithstanding Hunnicutt's proposal, the negroes voted for an immediate adjournment.[51] In this and in all other radical conventions throughout the reconstruction, it was very difficult to keep the blacks in order; at times they could not be controlled even by their most popular leaders.

This convention marks an era in the development of politics in the State of Virginia. The negroes finally decided against all conservative control and willfully rebuffed the Virginians who wished to act with them. It was unfortunate, but natural for them in their ignorance, that they should accept the alluring promises of the agitators rather than the smaller assurances of the "coöperators." So they cast in their lot with the radicals in the hope of gaining equality. The coöperation movement came to an abrupt end. The coöperators were disgusted with the insult-

---

[50] Fredericksburg News, August 2, 1867.

[51] Richmond Enquirer, August 3, 1867, and Dispatch of the same date.

ing treatment they had received[52] and the greater part of them returned to the conservative ranks. A few joined the Republican party, radical as its policy had become; among these was Judge Alexander Rives of Albemarle county. John Minor Botts also accepted the radical position and adhered to it through the short remainder of his political career.[53]

The tumultuous and confused August convention gave the conservative press a fair opportunity for renewed assaults upon the radicals and the negroes.[54] The conduct of the latter had been narrowly watched. They had ill acquitted themselves in their new dignity;[55] and the criticism was bitter.[56] But whatever effect it had upon the white people, the convention greatly increased the independence of the freedmen. Some of the Union Leagues even refused to admit whites as members.[57] In some places armed negro organizations were formed,[58] to the fear of the people, and exaggeration increased the fear. Talk and expectation ran high.[59] The campaign was very vigorously conducted by the radical party and its orators succeeded in rousing the negroes so thoroughly that almost their entire strength was regis-

---

[52] Enquirer, August 29, 1867. [53] Enquirer, February 28, 1868.

[54] Enquirer, August 3, 1867: "The disgusting and loathsome exhibition of the past week demonstrates to the plainest intellect that the fate of Hayti awaits Virginia if, through apathy and indifference, the Caucasian majority in this State permit the African minority to obtain the control of the government. Completely demoralized and corrupted by the infamous renegades who have affiliated with them, a large portion of the negroes are now inaccessible to reason. If there were not, fortunately, in Virginia a large majority of white men, to whose instincts of race and interests we may be permitted to look hopefully, our prospects would be no better than those of Hayti when French radicalism kindled in that unhappy land the fires of servile insurrection. . . . The recent hideous radical carnival in this city, like a fire-bell at midnight, should arouse every honest white man in Virginia to a sense of danger."

[55] Richmond Whig, August 3, 1867.

[56] Charlottesville Chronicle, August, 1867.

[57] Enquirer, September 6, 1867.

[58] Enquirer, November 13, 1867. Fredericksburg News, August 15, 1867. Ex. Docs., 2nd session, 39th Congress, No. 72. Order of May 14, 1867. [59] Enquirer, October 31, 1867.

tered.[60] On the other hand, the conservatives lacked enthusiasm and energy.[61] The press, it is true, urged the people to register, but there was great apathy and the whites had no effective organization. The new party which was growing up under the name of Conservative was rather a general movement of opposition to radicalism than an organized party with definite aims.

Meanwhile registration was carried on throughout the State under the strict eye of military authority.[62] Congressional acts excluded many Confederates from voting and practically all of them from office, for the "test-oath" was required of all office-holders. Indeed, in many parts of the State the order excluded from governmental positions all who were competent to fill them. General Schofield announced that he would fill the vacancies,[63] and that disloyal officers would be removed and their places filled by appointment. Many men were thereupon dismissed, and the vacant positions were given to Unionists. An officer of General Schofield's staff was assigned to the judgeship of the Richmond hustings court.[64] On account of the lack of available men, offices were often given to carpet-baggers, who were usually entirely unfitted for their duties.

The military authority exercised very wide and varying powers under the reconstruction acts. General Schofield announced by order of May 28, 1867, that for the purpose of giving protection in cases where the civil authorities might fail, military commissioners should be selected from the army and the Freedmen's Bureau. These commission-

---

[60] Ex. Docs., 2nd session, 39th Congress, No. 72. [61] Ibid.

[62] By General Order No. 34, all persons who had held civil or military offices under the United States, and those who had held State, legislative, executive or judicial offices and had given aid to the Confederacy, were disfranchised. The act of Congress of July 9, 1867, named the "test-oath" as a qualification for office. This oath was the same as that required by the Federal government of its officers. It declared that the subscriber had not engaged in armed revolt against the United States. [63] Order of July 26, 1867.

[64] Appleton's Annual Cyclopædia, 1867, p. 762. Enquirer, September 18, 1867.

ers were given jurisdiction over sub-districts with military forces to sustain them, and were also placed in command of the police of cities and the power of counties for the purpose of suppressing insurrection and violence. For the protection of individuals commissioners were given the authority of county justices or police magistrates, with the direction to conform to the laws of Virginia as far as they did not conflict with those of the United States. Further, it was the duty of commissioners to report all cases and their decisions to headquarters. Trials by civil courts were preferred when justice would probably be done; otherwise the commissioners should intervene and conduct them.[65] An order of September 21, 1867, authorized the sub-commissioners to exercise the jurisdiction given by the law to a judge of the State circuit court.[66] Interference by the military authorities in matters of justice became fairly common, and decisions of the State courts were frequently annulled. There were some hundreds of cases of this sort. One such was that of C. C. Ball vs. Daniel Malone in Norfolk, in which the decision of the local court was set aside by an order of August 6, 1867.[67]

The campaign increased in warmth as the nominations for delegates to the convention were made. The negroes for the time gave themselves up to politics, for which they had already acquired an extreme liking. The difficulty of obtaining labor was consequently great in some sections, as the blacks lived in constant attendance upon political meetings. The freedmen showed a considerable aptitude for politics and demanded and received a share of the nominations. They gave an enthusiastic support to all the radical measures, especially confiscation.[68]

The campaign of 1867 came to a close in October. All

---

[65] Appleton's Annual Cyclopædia, 1867, p. 759.
[66] Report of Secretary of War, 40th Congress, 2nd session, Vol. 1, p. 240.
[67] The Special Order Book, Military Department No. 1, at the State Library, Richmond.
[68] Enquirer, April 19, 1867; April 27 and May 13, 1867.

through the State candidates were nominated for the convention. About one-third of the radical nominees were negroes; this basis of representation seems to have been agreed upon, although sometimes the proportion of negro candidates was larger. At the meeting in Fredericksburg two whites and one negro were chosen. It was resolved "That our candidates must pledge themselves to sustain the principles of the Union Republican party, especially the equal political rights of all men in all respects; a system of common schools in which no distinctions shall be made on account of color and race, a general provision for the poor and a just and equitable system of taxation."[69] This seems to have been a fairly representative platform.

In Richmond an effort was made by the more conservative Republicans to have a prominent and representative man nominated for that city.[70] The names of Governor Peirpont and Franklin Stearns, an influential Republican, were proposed. The radical leaders, however, refused to consider the candidacy of more conservative men. The nominating convention was held on October 13, and there was a great gathering of negroes in the Capitol Square.[71] The tobacco factories closed for the day, in order to give the workmen a chance to attend. The radicals were in complete control of the great assembly and directed its choice. Judge Underwood, J. W. Hunnicutt and James Morrissey, an Irishman, with two negroes, Lewis Lindsay and James Cox, were nominated.[72] Morrissey was selected in place of Governor Peirpont or Franklin Stearns. The conservative Republicans, disappointed in the chosen candidates, considered the advisability of forming a separate ticket. Accordingly, they attempted to hold a meeting, but it was broken up by the mob of radical freedmen in hot

[69] Fredericksburg News, September, 1867.
[70] Ibid., October 17, 1867.
[71] "It was composed of men, women and children, and attended by the inevitable peddlers of cakes, lemonade, fried fish, stale gingerbread and starch candy in large numbers."—Fredericksburg News, October 17.
[72] Enquirer, October 15, 1867.

anger at the dissenters.[73] The plan was then abandoned, as it had become very evident that the moderate leaders could count on little support from the colored population.[74]

The State registration, when completed, showed a total of 225,933 voters, of whom 120,101 were white and 105,832 colored. The former were, therefore, considerably in the majority, but under the system of representation adopted they could hardly hope to elect a majority of the delegates.[75] Many conservative papers accused the military authorities of gerrymandering the State in the radical interest, but there seems to have been little ground for this charge. For it is evident from the statistics that the vote was so distributed, that while there was a white majority and a majority of white counties, many more voters lived in the counties having black majorities than in the white. The negro population was far more concentrated, giving it a decided advantage.

The election was held on October 18-21, 1867. In Richmond the polls were kept open three days,[76] and far into the night of the third, in order to give the negroes an opportunity to poll a full vote. There was disorder in some places, and troops dispersed a mob at Richmond.[77] The

---

[73] Enquirer, October 15, 1867.

[74] The Richmond Whig abandoned the Republican party for the time being. On October 21, it said: "There are but two tickets before the people of Richmond—the run-mad radical and the conservative tickets. It is now too late for any other to be presented. Between these two the people of Richmond will have to make their choice."

[75] Report of Secretary of War, 40th Congress, 2nd session, Vol. 1, p. 294. The white majority was 14,269. The whites were more numerous in 52 counties and the blacks in 50. The aggregate number of voters, however, in the white districts was 90,555 to an aggregate of 125,895 in the black districts. Each delegate represented 2,061 constituents. According to the report of the military authorities, the aggregate representation would have given 44 delegates elected in white districts to 61 in black. The actual apportionment allowed 47 white districts and 58 negro. The report further stated that on the basis of representation in the State senate there would have been 42 delegates from 22 white districts, and 18 black districts would elect 58 delegates. Congressional representation would have given 34 white and 71 colored delegates.

[76] Enquirer, October 24, 1867.

[77] Ibid.

freedmen showed great enthusiasm; it is said that in Richmond county they began to come to the polls by midnight, and by nine or ten o'clock in the morning all had voted.[78]

The victory lay with the radical party. It elected 72 delegates, 25 of whom were negroes, to 33 conservatives. The whites cast 76,084 votes; the blacks 93,145. The apathy of the conservative people is evident in the fact that 44,000 registered white men failed to vote. The poll for the convention was 107,342; against it, 61,887; 14,835 whites voted for it and 638 blacks against.[79] The last figure shows how united the negro race had become in the radical party. Fraud [80] and intimidation [81] were charged by the conservative press, especially in the election at Richmond. It is difficult to ascertain the truth. The newspapers also criticized Schofield for keeping the polls open in Richmond after the three appointed days had passed. He said, in reply, that he had done so on account of the crowd, which prevented some from voting. This excuse is not very plausible, perhaps, in view of the consideration that the election lasted three days, yet there seems small ground for charging the military with dishonest intention. The Richmond Whig even asserted that General Schofield desired the defeat of the Hunnicutt ticket in Richmond.[82] But in any case the result was too decisive to have been brought about by manipulation.

Indeed, the conservatives were dismayed by the magnitude of their defeat.[83] The bitterness of the beaten party found vent in the discharge of negro employees for voting the radical ticket.[84] On the other hand, the radical leaders became more violent in their expressions, possibly because of

---

[78] Fredericksburg News, November 7, 1867.

[79] Ex. Docs., 2nd session, 40th Congress, No. 342. Order of November 2, 1867.

[80] Enquirer, February 4, 1868. [81] Enquirer, November 21, 1867.

[82] Fredericksburg News, November 4, 1867.

[83] Whig, October 25, 1867.

[84] Lynchburg Virginian, quoted by Fredericksburg News, November 7, 1867. Enquirer, December 16, 1867.

their success. Finally Hunnicutt was arrested November 27, on a warrant issued by a Charles City justice, charging him with inciting the negroes of that county to insurrection and race war. The military authority intervened and ordered him to be released on bail.[85]

The result of the election had shown the conservatives the imperative need for a thorough party organization. Accordingly the executive committee of the conservative party of Richmond, including members of the old Whig and Democratic central executive committees, issued a call for a State convention to be held in Richmond on December 11, 1867. The press throughout the State, more hostile than ever to the radical party, gave hearty support.

About 800 delegates met in convention at Richmond on the eleventh of December.[86] Every part of Virginia was represented by prominent and influential men, among whom were John B. Baldwin, A. H. H. Stuart, J. R. Branch, R. M. T. Hunter, Thomas S. Bocock, John Letcher, T. H. Flournoy, Ex-Governor Kemper, James Barbour, Col. Randolph and others.

Alexander H. H. Stuart was elected president. He opened the discussions of the convention in a significant speech. "At the close of the war," he said, "we were assured that upon the repeal of the ordinance of secession, the repudiation of the Confederate debt and emancipation of the slaves, we would be restored to our rights in the Union; but instead of these promises being fulfilled, a policy has been inaugurated placing the Southern States under the control of our inferior race. We have met to appeal to the North not to permit the infliction of this disgrace upon us. Our rights may be wrested from us, but we will never submit to the rule of an alien and inferior race. We prefer the rule of the bayonet. . . . We desire further to perfect our organization so that all who desire that this shall continue to

---

[85] Richmond Enquirer, November 29, 1867.
[86] Enquirer and Whig, December 12, 1867.

be a white man's government may be able to act in concert and by one vigorous and united effort save ourselves from ruin and disgrace." [87]

Resolutions were adopted stating: (1) That slavery had been abolished and that it was not the purpose of the Virginia people to reduce the negroes again to that condition. (2) That Virginia should be restored to the Union. (3) That the people of Virginia were entitled to the rights provided by the Constitution of the United States. (4) That "to subject the white people of the State to the absolute supremacy, in their local government, in their representation in the senate and house of delegates, to the black race just emerged from personal servitude is abhorrent to the civilization of mankind." (5) The convention further declared that it disclaimed all hostility to the freedmen, but held that the white race should rule the State.

A complex system of party organization was adopted.[88] First, there was to be a State committee of 35 members, nine of them residents of Richmond. The chief director was the chairman of the committee. Besides, there were eight associate directors and 24 consulting members from the eight Congressional districts. Voters should be organized in tens and fifties under the supervision of the superintendents of districts. R. T. Daniel, Marmaduke Johnson, H. K. Ellyson, M D. Coleman, Robert Ould, T. J. Evans, J. C. Shields, J. R. Fisher and J. R. Branch were appointed as members of the central committee. This system seems rather cumbrous and was not carried out in all its details, but the greatly increased strength of the conservative party in the next election was due, in part, to its better organization.

---

[87] Enquirer, December 12, 1867. [88] Enquirer, December 13, 1867.

## CHAPTER VI.

### THE CONSTITUTIONAL CONVENTION OF 1868.

The constitutional convention assembled in the capitol in Richmond on December 3, 1867.[1] It was composed of 105 members. The radicals had elected 72 delegates and the conservatives 33, but several members elected by the Republicans identified themselves with the conservatives, thus making them about one-half the number of their opponents.

This convention was the most remarkable political assembly that ever met in Virginia. It was the first legislative body in the history of the State in which negroes sat as members. For this reason and on account of the bitter political feeling of the time, the session of the convention was exceedingly inharmonious. The membership of the body indicates the great political revolution that had taken place in Virginia with the extension of the ballot to the colored race. The old, long-dominant planter class, which had governed the State through its previous history, was now without power; the organic law was to be framed by negroes and the white representatives of negroes and of the whites who supported the Republican party in defiance of their race. The radical majority was composed of twenty-five negroes and about forty-five white men. Fourteen of the latter were native Virginians; the others came from Northern States and a few from abroad.[2] The majority was

[1] Enquirer, December 4, 1867.

[2] According to the address of the conservative members (see Fredericksburg News, April 23, 1867) there were on the radical side, 24 negroes, 14 native white Virginians, 13 New Yorkers, one member each from Pennsylvania, Ohio, Maine, Vermont, Connecticut, South Carolina, Maryland and the District of Columbia; two from England and one each from Ireland, Scotland, Nova Scotia and Canada.

dominated by the political ideas that then held the popular mind in the North. These humanitarian and democratic theories made no allowance for the great differences of condition existing between the two races. Consequently it was evident that there would be difficulty in finding such a ground of compromise between the radicals and the conservatives as would allow both parties to take part in forming the new constitution. In fact, no meeting place was found and the radicals alone framed the constitution, while the conservatives became a mere party of obstruction.

The convention, immediately upon assembling, proceeded to the election of officers.[3] Judge John C. Underwood was elected president, receiving 64 votes to the 33 for the Reverend Norval Wilson, the conservative candidate.

John Curtiss Underwood was born in Litchfield, New York, in 1808.[4] He removed to Virginia some years before the Civil War, but afterwards left the State on account of the unpopularity he incurred from his abolitionist sentiments. The Washington government made him the district judge of Virginia in 1861. He established his court in Alexandria and actively advocated the confiscation of Confederate property. After the war he went to Richmond, and the trial of Jefferson Davis fell within his jurisdiction. Indeed, a jury, composed of blacks as well as of whites, had been impaneled when Davis was admitted to bail. Underwood derived his importance entirely from his position as a Federal judge, and he was elected president of the convention on this account.

The convention of 1868 was remarkable in that none of the well-known politicians of Virginia took part in it, their places being filled by young men, who now for the first time came into public notice. The ablest debater on the floor

---

[3] Judge Snead of Accomac received three votes, H. M. Bowden, one. Other officers were George Rye, secretary; J. H. Painter and W. J. Hunter, assistant secretaries; W. R. Tall, sergeant-at-arms; W. H. Samuel, official reporter. Debates 7.

[4] Appleton's Cyclopædia of American Biography, Vol. 6, p. 210.

was John L. Marye, Jr., of Fredericksburg. The most aggressive conservative leader was Eustace Gibson of Giles. James M. French, J. C. Gibson, Jacob W. Liggett, W. H. Robertson and Norval Wilson were also prominent men on this side.

Judge John C. Underwood, Judge Edward Snead, John Hawxhurst, James W. Hunnicutt, Charles H. Porter, Edgar Allan, James H. Clements, James H. Platt, Orrin E. Hine, David B. White and Henry M. Bowden were the radical leaders. The most distinguished negro members were Dr. Thomas Bayne, Willis A. Hodges and Lewis Lindsay. Edward Snead of Accomac was the ablest debater on the Republican side. He was a fair-minded and logical man, more moderate in his opinions than the majority of his party. The negroes proved apt pupils in the school of politics. Although entirely ignorant at first, they soon acquired a knowledge of the rules of legislative proceedings, which they delighted to apply, rising on all possible occasions to "pints" of order.[5] They spoke poor English, of course, but were nothing daunted by this drawback; indeed Dr. Bayne became the most garrulous speaker in the convention.[6]

The first few weeks of the session were mainly spent in organization and in preliminary political discussions.[7] From the very first party lines were drawn. The conservatives, in view of the great impoverishment of the State, did not wish to expend much money upon the convention. The radicals, on the other hand, realized its importance and favored a more liberal expenditure, especially as some of them were adventurers from outside the State. The convention finally adopted a per diem of eight dollars.[8] The Republicans inclined to take a large view of the powers of the convention, and presented a very wide range of reso-

---

[5] History of Augusta County, p. 350. Enquirer, February 7, 1868.

[6] Enquirer, March 25, 1868. Mr. Parr wished to limit him to five speeches a day.

[7] Debates of Convention, p. 42 et seq.

[8] Debates, p. 41.

lutions and petitions; even practical legislation was proposed which lay beyond the legitimate sphere of a constitutional convention.[9]

Nothing, however, came of the attempts of some inexperienced members to stretch the powers of the constitutional convention so as to include those of the general assembly. By January the committees had been organized and they then settled down to their tasks. The period of disconnected resolutions and discussions passed away; and the public work of the convention began in earnest as the constitution was referred by parts from the various committees. The radicals displayed their political philosophy as practically applied in the various reforms and changes they proposed to make in the organic law of Virginia.[10]

On January 6, 1868, the committee on the preamble and the bill of rights brought in its report.[11] The first section of the preamble was the same as in the old constitution.[12] Various substitutes were offered[13] by the conservatives and radicals. The most sweeping change proposed was that of James White, who wished to do away with the old preamble altogether.[14] J. W. D. Bland offered a resolution striking out the word "men" from the first section as reported and inserting in its place the words "mankind, irrespective of race or color." But this amendment, intended for the protection of the colored race, was strongly opposed by the negro members, because it made a specific reference to racial differences, while the negroes were bent on keeping out of the new constitution any reference whatever to race

[9] An injunction was asked to prevent the lease of the Norfolk ferry.

[10] Namely, distinction between the races on steamboats, on railroads, on street-cars and in schools.

[11] Debates p. 221.

[12] Debates, p. 241. "That all men are by nature equally free and independent and have certain inherent rights of which when they enter into a state of society, they cannot, by any compact, deprive or divest their posterity,—namely, the enjoyment of life and liberty, with the means of acquiring and possessing property, and obtaining happiness and safety."

[13] P. 241, 246.

[14] P. 248.

distinctions.[15] The section reported by the committee was finally adopted.

On January 8, the second section of the bill of rights as reported came up for discussion.[16] This clause, which declared that the first allegiance of the citizen was due to the Federal government, naturally stirred up a lively debate. The conservatives objected to a declaration of entire supremacy on the part of the United States, while the Republicans wished to embody the results of the war in such a specific declaration as would make secession impossible in the future.[17] The discussion upon this subject became somewhat bitter. Finally a more moderate substitute, offered by Thomas, for the second article of the report was adopted.[18]

After the adoption of the bill of rights, the convention proceeded to the consideration of those specific questions in which were embodied the reconstruction of Virginia. James H. Clements presented the report of the committee on taxation on January 15. This report marked a new period in the deliberations of the convention, as the question of taxation held its attention for a great part of the session. The report recommended that (1) taxation should be equal and uniform throughout the State, and all property should be taxed in proportion to its value. (2) No tax should be imposed for taking oysters except for those taken and planted in private beds. (3) The general assembly might

---

[15] Debates, p. 251. Bayne said: "I pledged the good people of my section that I should endeavor to aid in making a constitution that should not have the word black or the word white anywhere in it."

[16] P. 261. "That the authority of the General Government of the United States is paramount to that of an individual State, except as to rights guaranteed to each State by the Constitution of the United States; and that, therefore, the first allegiance of a citizen of any State is due to the General Government."

[17] P. 262 et seq.

[18] Thomas's substitute, p. 265, "That the Constitution of the United States, and the laws of Congress passed in pursuance thereof, constitute the supreme law of the land, to which paramount allegiance and obedience are due from every citizen, anything in the constitution, ordinances or laws of any State to the contrary notwithstanding."

levy a tax on incomes over $1000, and on certain licenses—the sale of spirits, lotteries, peddlers, theatrical exhibitions and businesses which could not be reached by the ad valorem system. Capital invested in business should be taxed as other property. (4) The general assembly might levy a poll-tax on males over twenty-one years of age, not exceeding the assessment on $500 worth of property, the proceeds of which were to be applied to education.

There was unquestionably a need of reform in the methods of taxation, especially in those of the local levies. To the first section of the report, which declared that taxation should be equal and uniform throughout the State, H. M. Bowden offered an amendment inserting after the word "taxation" the words "imposed by the State, county or corporal bodies." Radical members, in support of this resolution, pointed out the abuses in the system of county levies that then existed in Virginia. These varied very greatly in different counties. The tendency in certain parts of the State was to throw the burden of local taxation largely upon the polls and to lay a very light tax on real property.[19] This was to some extent justified by the destitute condition of many land-holders, but the system was carried too far. James H. Platt asserted that the county of Prince George levied a $6 poll-tax; Bowden, that the poll-tax in Norfolk was $5; and similar instances were cited. After some discussion, Bowden's amendment was adopted.

The third section of the report on taxation granted the legislature power to levy an income tax and also to lay licenses upon a few limited classes of employment.[20] Doctors, lawyers and other professions and callings were exempt from the payment of license according to this section. This policy was an innovation in Virginia legislation and exceptions were taken to the report by several members.

---

[19] John Hawxhurst said: "Some counties that I know of laid a tax of ten cents on the hundred dollars' worth of property, and a tax of over three dollars on the head, five and six in some cases."—Debates, p. 651.

[20] Debates, p. 665.

William L. Owen pointed out the deficiencies of the proposed law, in leaving untouched many kinds of business which should properly be taxed.[21] In fact the radicals wished to practically exempt all trades from burdens and to greatly lighten poll-taxes; in order to encourage laborers and small tradesmen, and especially to throw the weight of taxation upon land. They claimed that the agricultural interests had imposed heavy licenses upon all possible callings, for the purpose of exempting the plantations, and that this policy had tended to the injury of the commerce and manufactures of Virginia. James Curtiss declared that one of the reasons for the greater prosperity of the Northern States lay in their system of taxing values rather than occupations, which system greatly encouraged the industrial callings.[22] Furthermore, the radicals thought that by throwing the chief taxation upon real property, the large land-holders would be forced to sell their estates, which lay idle under the existing light taxation. The result would be to the advantage of the poor man, especially the negro, for at that time planters were unwilling to sell part of their holdings to the small buyers. The third section of the report was adopted by a vote of 58 to 34.[23]

Another most important measure was the institution of public schools. This question had been considered by the Alexandria legislature and the Alexandria constitutional convention of 1864, but these bodies, for lack of any real power, had not accomplished anything. But public education was one of the main features of the radical reconstruction policy and now received due attention in the Virginia convention.

The report of the committee on education provided for the establishment of free schools throughout the State. This report, which was drawn up on the responsibility of the radical majority in the committee, was adopted. The

---

[21] He enumerated twenty or thirty such occupations. Debates, p. 666.

[22] Debates, p. 678.

[23] Debates, p. 726.

credit for the establishment of popular education, therefore, rests with the Republican party and this great service rendered to Virginia outweighs much of the extravagance of the radical propaganda.

But in this notable and laudable institution lurked the possibility of a perilous social disturbance. The conservatives realized the danger, and James French at once moved to amend the report on education so that white and colored children should be educated entirely apart.[25] But his amendment offended the negro members and was lost by a party vote of 21 to 37. Indeed, the blacks were bent on defeating any attempt to establish separate schools for the two races, rightly estimating the immense social importance of education, and the increased consideration that would come to the colored people under a system of indiscriminate education. Dr. Bayne introduced an amendment providing that free schools should be open to all without distinction of color. His resolution was lost, many white radical members voting against it. Lewis Lindsay then declared that if this right was not granted he would warn all carpet-baggers to pack up and leave Virginia.[26] He assured them that his race did not intend to be hobby-horses to ride them into office, and gave notice that if a provision for mixed schools was not placed in the constitution, nine-tenths of the negroes in Virginia would vote against its adoption. Willis Hodges announced that if a division in the Republican party was necessary, the question of mixed schools marked the proper place for that division; that the negroes insisted upon mixed schools. But a majority of the white Republicans clearly saw that the people of Virginia would not endure such a measure, and, in spite of the angry protests of the colored members, refused to insert a provision for mixed schools in the constitution.

---

[25] Enquirer, March 28. James Curtiss offered a substitute to provide text-books for poor children, which was adopted. Thereupon E. Gibson brought in the sarcastic resolution, "and also provide baskets and buckets for the children to carry their dinners to school in."—Enquirer, March 30.

[26] Enquirer, April 8, 1868.

The leading political question of the reconstruction was that of suffrage. It applied not only to the advisability of conferring the voting franchise upon the colored race, but also to the wisdom of the exclusion of certain classes of Confederates from that privilege. Consequently there was wide latitude for variety of opinion and extremity of antagonism. Suffrage was brought before the Virginia convention at an early period and was fiercely debated until the very last day of the session.

The seventh section of the bill of rights as reported by the committee stated "That all elections ought to be free and that all men, having sufficient evidence of permanent common interest with and attachment to the community, have the right of suffrage," etc. John Hawxhurst moved to amend and insert the words, "That all elections ought to be free and that all men should have the right of suffrage."[27] This amendment embodied the extreme radical attitude in the matter of suffrage, for it asserted that suffrage was a natural right. It was promptly attacked by several Republicans, Clements, Platt and Snead, and by the conservative, Eustace Gibson. Snead opposed the doctrine of the inherent right of suffrage, which Hawxhurst advocated, and pointed out the fact that under the constitution a natural right was inalienable, if it were a natural right. Hawxhurst's amendment was defeated and the seventh section of the bill of rights was adopted as reported.

But although the radicals refused to consider suffrage as a natural right, they proposed to confer the privilege of voting and of office-holding upon the colored race. Judge Underwood, on January 16, 1868, offered a resolution[28] granting these privileges not only to negroes but to women as well. He supported the resolution in a speech of great length, asserting that three classes of citizens had been formerly deprived of some of their rights in Virginia—the

---

[27] Debates, p. 343.

[28] Debates, p. 458. Richmond Enquirer and Richmond Dispatch, January 17, 1868.

clergy, negroes and women. This speech is a typical example of the extreme radical doctrines of the day, but Underwood's views in regard to female suffrage were too advanced to please the majority of the Republicans, and, indeed, he had very little real influence with them. The president's frankly abusive address naturally stirred up the conservative members. Marye answered him in an excellent speech, arguing that the negroes should apply themselves to their crying economic needs rather than to injurious political agitation.[29]

This debate on suffrage extended over some days. Hawxhurst renewed his effort to have suffrage declared as a natural right. "It is an inherent and God-given right of man," he says; "he does not obtain it through any set of men." Eustace Gibson ridiculed this theory of the "inherent right" of suffrage. The negroes, however, warmly supported this doctrine, as it, of course, strengthened their claims to suffrage, and Dr. Bayne made several speeches in support of Hawxhurst's amendment. But Underwood, Hunnicutt and Snead opposed it and the amendment was rejected. Some of the radicals persisted in the desire to have all the political rights declared as natural rights. Notwithstanding the defeat of such amendments, Charles Porter introduced a resolution, stating that voting, office-holding and jury-service should be open to all. He declared that jury-service was a right. Judge Snead denied this strongly. "You might as well say that a man has the right to pay taxes," he said. Jury-service was not a right but a burden. Nevertheless, from the point of view of the negro, Porter was not far wrong. The most strenuous efforts were made by the radicals to have this burden imposed upon the very willing freedmen. Judge Underwood

[29] "Instead of teaching them (negroes) . . . to depend upon their own honest labors for their livelihood, their minds have been beguiled and deluded to thinking that they may live without labor and thrive without effort . . . What will your experiment bring when you are teaching that class that honor, profit, emolument and dignity should be their present goal and aspiration."

summoned negroes for the juries in his court. It would have been an immense stride for the freedmen in the consideration of the world, if they had been able to gain the privilege of sitting upon juries, but they were utterly unfit for the duty and their claims never received the serious consideration of the State courts.

The convention grew more turbulent as the session wore on. Especially was this the case when the question of suffrage was brought up for its final settlement. It now occupied the attention of the convention for the greater part of the remainder of the term. The meetings were sometimes very stormy, and members came almost to blows. The temper of the conservative press grew more and more denunciatory, as it became increasingly evident that the radical members intended to embody sweeping measures of disfranchisment in the constitution.[30]

The majority report of the committee on suffrage advocated the disfranchisement of those classes of citizens already disfranchised by the reconstruction act, together with certain new classes. The minority report, drawn up by John L. Marye, called attention to the defects of this plan. It stated that the article proposed by the majority of the committee would confer the right of suffrage upon all adult male negroes, not excepting paupers, while it would exclude many white men. All negroes might also hold office and sit upon juries, while the disfranchised white citizens could not. All voting would be by ballot, a form not then popular in Virginia. The oath to be taken by the voter required the recognition of the civil and political equality of all men, an oath to which no conscientious conservative could subscribe. The minority report further declared that no republican government could succeed unless the electors

[30] The Richmond Enquirer said on February 12: "Will the patience of the Northern people allow this monstrosity much longer? It is not merely an absurdity. It is not merely a disgust. It is a terror. It is that most diabolical of plots and of dramas—a frightful tragedy in the garb of a farce . . . It gives to republican forms their deadliest blow by making them supremely contemptible."

possessed intelligence, moral culture and a property stake,[31] in all of which the colored race was deficient. James French, conservative, although in favor of the minority report, was willing to accept impartial qualified suffrage as the next best thing.[32] This was the general desire of the conservative members. On the other hand, radical expressions became more pronounced. Hunnicutt declared that the constitution would probably be rejected by the popular vote, and, therefore, he was in favor of disfranchising 30,000 more men in addition to those already disfranchised.[33]

The minority report was rejected by a decisive vote upon March 4,[34] and the majority report was then taken up for consideration. It provided that all male citizens twenty-one years of age might vote, with the following exceptions: lunatics, persons convicted of felony, treason or bribery, duelists and all persons disfranchised by the fourteenth amendment or the reconstruction act. A two-thirds vote of both houses of the legislature might re-enfranchise. The first three sections of the report were adopted without much debate.

But the hottest fight of the whole convention raged about the fourth section. Orrin E. Hine offered a subsitute disfranchising every Confederate who had been a Senator, Congressman, Presidential elector; who had held any civil or military office under the United States or under any State, and who had taken the oath of allegiance to the United States.[35] This practically included all the officers in the State.[36] Snead proposed an amendment to the sub-

---

[31] According to this report, the returns from fifteen counties in Virginia showed that in these counties the negroes owned only $139.09 worth of taxable property and the greater part of their poll-tax was unpaid.—Enquirer, February 28, 1868.

[32] Enquirer, February 26, 1868.

[33] Enquirer and Richmond Dispatch, March 4, 1868.

[34] Enquirer, March 5. [35] Enquirer, March 7, 1868, and Dispatch.

[36] Eustace Gibson wished, in return, to offer the following sarcastic resolution: "No man shall vote or hold office who can support himself and family," but he was ruled out of order.—Enquirer, March 7, 1868.

stitute, to the effect that voting for the ordinance of secession or acts of charity to Confederate soldiers should not be regarded as rebellion. The amendment was lost, 35 to 52. Hine's substitute was adopted, 49 to 28.

Hine next offered an amendment, as the fifth clause of the first section, which disfranchised every Confederate officer above the rank of first lieutenant in the army and master in the navy. It was adopted by a vote of 53 to 35.

It was felt in Congress that Hine's disfranchising measures were too sweeping,[37] as the new amendment would probably have disfranchised several thousand more men. Accordingly the Republican leaders in Congress intimated to the radical members of the convention that they had gone too far in the matter of disfranchisement;[38] and a motion to reconsider Hine's amendment[39] was carried on March 12. The section of the report, with other amendments, was then passed. Hine offered still another substitute disfranchising all persons who had voted for candidates to the secession convention advocating secession, and all persons who in any way had advocated secession prior to April 1, 1865.[40] This, however, did not include Confederate soldiers who had laid down their arms before January 1, 1865. The substitute was lost by a vote of 36 to 47.

Hunnicutt then proposed for the fifth section a substitute which disfranchised all persons who had contracted for the Confederate government and had thereby been exempt from military service. This was lost.[41] Hawxhurst wished to disfranchise all who had advocated secession before April 17, 1861, or who had engaged in guerilla warfare, or had treated prisoners of war badly, or had been engaged in

---

[37] "The negroes and the New England squatters in the capitol have at last hoisted the black flag. There is no longer the slightest attempt upon their part to disguise the fact that the proscription and pillage of the white race are their object."—Enquirer, March 9, 1868.

[38] Kelso's speech. Enquirer, March 9, Enquirer, March 25, 1868.

[39] Richmond Dispatch and Enquirer March 13.

[40] Ibid.

[41] Enquirer and Dispatch, March 13.

conscript service, or had induced men to join the Confederate army by threats. This resolution did not pass.[42] Southall offered an amendment to the disfranchising section of the report which provided that no persons should be excluded by it, except those who had held the offices especially enumerated therein. The conservatives, however, could not obtain even this modification.[43]

Hine's disfranchising resolution was again brought before the convention. He was a man of strong convictions and force of will, and did all in his power to carry through a stringent measure of suffrage restriction. He received the earnest support of the negroes, who were always advocates of extreme measures, but the white Republican members feared to push measures too far, especially against the wishes of Congress, which disapproved of a wholesale disfranchisement of Confederates. At length, Edgar Allan moved to postpone the subject of disfranchisement indefinitely. His motion passed, although the negroes longed for the opportunity to "make treason odious."[44] The attempt to extend disfranchisement came to an end.

The closing days of the convention found it once more concerned with suffrage. There was now a wish among many of the white radicals to soften the disfranchising measures of the constitution. They saw that it would be totally unacceptable to the people, unless its severities were modified. Snead offered a resolution to re-enfranchise all persons who had advocated the reconstruction act. The amendment was lost. James Platt wished to relieve mayors and councilmen of the necessity of taking the "iron-clad" oath. Other motions of exemption were made. It was evident that a part of the Republicans were becoming weary of the "iron-clad" oath and wished to strike it out of the constitution. But Hine continued firm in its support and commanded the allegiance of the negroes, so that every motion to reconsider, suspend or strike out was voted down.

---

[42] Enquirer and Dispatch, March 14.
[43] Ibid.
[44] Enquirer, March 27, 1868.

General Schofield, who was strongly opposed to disfranchisement, addressed the convention on April 17.[45] His views were moderate and sensible. He objected to the "iron-clad" oath as a great hindrance to government. In many counties, he said, there were only one or two men capable of filling the local offices who could subscribe to the oath. He had no hesitation in declaring that it would be impossible to administer the government on this basis. He had not interfered with the convention before, but on this subject he thought the members were misinformed, and if the provision requiring the oath remained in the constitution, it would be fatal to it and probably to them. In consequence of this speech, some of the radical members moved to reconsider the whole subject of suffrage, but Hine objected, and the president decided that a two-thirds vote was necessary for reconsideration. A motion to suspend the rules was beaten, 26 to 32. Nothing more could be done and the constitution was adopted the same day, April 17, 1868, by a vote of 51 to 36. Several Republicans voted with the conservatives against its adoption.[46]

A constitution framed by radicals was not likely to meet the approval of the people of the State in any case, and this constitution embodied new and revolutionary ideas, implied as well as declared. In consequence the conservative press assailed it without reservation. The Underwood constitution contained the great measures of the Virginia reconstruction policy, but not the extreme radical views. Civil equality was guaranteed alike to whites and blacks, and all men, without distinction of color, might vote, hold office and sit on juries, provided they were sane and had not committed certain offenses. Idiots, felons and duelists were disfranchised; likewise "every person who has been a Senator or Representative in Congress, or elector of President or Vice-President, or who held any office, civil or military, under the United States, or under any State, who having

[45] Enquirer and Dispatch, April 18, 1868.
[46] Enquirer and Dispatch, April 18, 1868.

previously taken an oath as a member of Congress, or as an officer of the United States, or as a member of any State legislature, or as an executive or judicial officer of any State, shall have engaged in insurrection or rebellion against the same, or given aid or comfort to the enemies thereof." [47] The legislature, by a three-fifths vote of both houses, might remove the disabilities of this clause. Furthermore, all persons before entering upon office were required to take the "test-oath," to the effect that the subscriber had not voluntarily aided the Confederacy or held office under it. It will be seen that these were the disfranchising measures of the Federal government.

The "county organization" plan of the constitution also met with much condemnation.[48] It was felt that it was an unnecessary innovation in the Virginia system and that the division of counties into townships was a cumbrous and expensive arrangement. The township system has never been a success in Virginia, being unsuited to the sparse population of many sections of the State.

The plan of "county organization" provided for a public school system. Nothing was said about separate schools for whites and blacks. The negroes in the convention had fought long and hard to gain an explicit declaration in the constitution of the right of colored children to attend any schools, but the white radicals recognized the impossibility of securing this demand, in view of the opposition of the white people, and the blacks finally abandoned the attempt.

Taxation was made equal and uniform on different species of property. Licenses were limited to a few callings, chiefly of a transitory nature. But the restrictions on this form of taxation have not been entirely observed.

The constitution in other main features did not meet with the approval of the Conservative people. Indeed they generally condemned it, on the ground that no fundamental law could be acceptable which excluded the majority of the

---

[47] Article III, Section 4.

[48] Article VIII.

leading men in the State from political rights. The evident hostility of the white people to the constitution prevented its immediate submission to the popular vote for ratification. The Republican leaders paused in uncertainty, studying the political conditions in hopes of a favorable chance of acceptance. But none came for more than a year, and Virginia continued to live under military rule, which was more palatable to the people than the new constitution. The election upon it was finally held the next year, with the disfranchising clauses offered for rejection or acceptance apart from the main body. The constitution was adopted and the disfranchising articles rejected, and Virginia resumed her Federal relations. Thus shorn of proscriptive features, the constitution proved to be a pretty good one, in spite of the fact that "carpet-baggers" had assisted in making it. The Underwood constitution continued to be the organic law of the State from 1869 until 1902, when the present constitution was framed.

## CHAPTER VII.

### THE RESTORATION OF VIRGINIA.

While the constitutional convention was still in session, Governor Peirpont's administration came to an end. On April 4, 1867, General Schofield issued an order removing him from the governorship and appointing in his place General Henry H. Wells.[1] General Wells was a native of New York but had lived for many years in Michigan, whence he had come to Virginia in the early part of the Civil War. He served as provost-marshal of Alexandria.

The reason assigned for the removal of Peirpont was the expiration of his term of office. This does not seem plausible, however, in view of the fact that the government of Virginia was purely provisional, and that a new executive was appointed without regard to the constitution. In truth, Peirpont's influence, which had waned for a long time, was by this time entirely lost. Conservative newspapers charged that he was not sufficiently radical in his views to please the authorities, and this seems to have been the general opinion. Certainly Peirpont was not well identified with any party. His views were too conservative for him to lend hearty support to the more radical measures, although he upheld the necessity of acquiescing in negro suffrage and in the other privileges the freedmen had obtained. His compromising turn of mind led him to attempt to keep a certain balance which he would at times abandon under the force of circumstances. It must be remembered that his position was a singularly difficult one.[2] He had been sharply criticized by the conservative press, but now that he was

---

[1] Richmond Enquirer, April 5, 1868.
[2] Enquirer, April 27, 1868, and August 13, 1867.

gone his former critics admitted his many good qualities and his material services to Virginia.[3]

The appointment of General Wells to the governorship gave a death-blow to Mr. Hunnicutt's aspirations. His power had weakened considerably during the session of the constitutional convention, in which he showed little proof of constructive statesmanship, but he was yet popular with the negroes. Hunnicutt and John Hawxhurst both announced themselves as candidates for governor, as soon as the time of election was fixed by the convention, and both began an active canvass among the freedmen.[4] But it appeared that the rulers in Washington did not favor leaders whose influence was confined solely to the negro race. For the leadership of the Republican party in Virginia a man of greater consideration was needed; a man who might also gain influence with white voters. Partly for this reason Wells was elevated to the gubernatorial chair.[5] Besides, a growing antagonism had sprung up between the native white Republicans or those of long residence in the State—"scalawags"[6] as they were vulgarly called—and the adventuring carpet-baggers. The latter held the advantage, in that they were in possession of the Federal offices and also enjoyed more influence at Washington. The appointment of Wells was a decided victory for the carpet-baggers. They now gained a complete ascendancy in the Republican party and drew away the freedmen from Hunnicutt and their other old leaders.

Peirpont's removal marked the beginning of many official changes. A few days later John S. Calvert, the State treasurer, was dismissed on the charge of having retained State funds, and George Rye was appointed in his place.[7] The superintendent of the State prison was also removed, and on May 8, Joseph Mayo, the mayor of Richmond,

---

[3] Enquirer, April 6, 1868. [4] Enquirer, March 24 and 27, 1868.
[5] New Nation, April 14, 1868.
[6] Scalawag is said to be a term applied to the scaly, scabby runts in a herd of cattle. See also Enquirer, October 7, 1868.
[7] Appleton's Annual Cyclopædia, 1868, p. 761.

gave away to George Chahoon, the military appointee. On May 15, General Schofield wrote to General Grant that the number of State officers who could not retain their offices under the provisions of the "test-oath" would amount to several thousand and that only a small portion of the vacancies so created could be filled.[8]

General Schofield was himself removed from command of the district on June 1. General Stoneman succeeded. Schofield had filled a hard and difficult position to the satisfaction of a majority of the fair-minded people of Virginia. As a military administrator he had used his great powers with discretion and had not interfered much further in the affairs of the State than his orders directed. The military rule under Stoneman became more oppressive. This was partly due to the latter's more stringent orders. Congress, on February 6, 1869, passed a joint resolution directing the removal from office of all persons who were unable to take the "test-oath" of the act of July 2, 1862. Stoneman published the law on March 15. He reported on March 21 that there were 5,446 offices in the state, of which 532 had been filled by General Schofield and 1,972 by himself.[9] Only 329 of the incumbents could take the "test-oath" and 2,613 vacancies still existed. Great difficulty was experienced in finding competent men to fill public positions; in fact, the functions of local government were suspended in many parts of Virginia. Stoneman in turn lost his command on March 5 and General Canby was appointed his successor. He assumed control on April 20, remaining as commander of the district until the end of Virginia reconstruction.

The rival parties began to prepare for the coming election shortly after the close of the constitutional convention. The conservative State committee, on April 17, 1868, issued a call for a convention, to be held at Richmond on May 7. It should include the superintendents of counties

---

[8] Appleton's Annual Cyclopædia, 1868, p. 761.
[9] Appleton's Annual Cyclopædia, 1869, p. 710.

and cities, and the resident and consulting members of the State committee.[10]

The Republican State convention met at Richmond on May 6. There was a full attendance of delegates, every county sending a quota. Representation was about equally divided between the races. James H. Clements was elected president. General Wells, supported by the military power, received the nomination for governor. One hundred and fifty-three votes were cast for him; forty-five for Hawxhurst; eleven for Hunnicutt, and six for Peirpont. It will be seen how greatly Hunnicutt's influence had declined. Clements was nominated for the lieutenant-governorship.[11]

The conservative convention assembled the next day with eighty-four delegates present. Colonel R. E. Withers was nominated for governor, General James Walker for lieutenant-governor and John L. Marye, Jr., for attorney-general.[12]

The radicals now wished to make arrangements for the election. In June, Governor Wells and Judge H. G. Bond, one of his chief supporters, went to Washington and requested the reconstruction committee to provide for an immediate election in Virginia with an appropriation of money to pay expenses. They desired especially that the election might be held upon the existing registration.[13]

There was so general a feeling of hostility to the new constitution among the white people that a fresh registration would doubtless have brought out a full vote against its adoption. The House of Representatives passed a bill which fixed the date of the Virginia election as August 13, 14, 15, 1868. Wells objected to the bill on the ground that it re-opened registration and it was feared that many persons would attempt to register under the amnesty proclama-

---

[10] Enquirer, April 18, 1868. [11] Enquirer and Whig, May 7, 1868.

[12] Fredericksburg News, November 9, 1868. Nominations for Congress and for other offices were made at the same time. Carpetbaggers were generally selected by the Republicans, only one of their eight Congressional nominees being a Virginian.

[13] Fredericksburg News, July 16, 1868.

tion.[14] He accordingly went again to Washington and urged his views upon the reconstruction committee. These were so partisan that Mr. Beck of Kentucky attacked him in the House of Representatives; and largely through Beck's influence Congress gave no immediate response to his demands. The election remained suspended, therefore, through the whole year 1868.

In the first part of December the Republican State central committee of Virginia met in Richmond to consider the question of registration. Finally it was decided to ask Congress to continue the Freedmen's Bureau in the unreconstructed States, until they should be admitted to the rights of statehood, and to order an election on the constitution at the earliest possible day.

The committee also resolved to submit the whole of the constitution without exception to the voters, and a petition asking such action on the part of Congress was prepared and signed by many leading Republicans of the State, including Governor Wells, Judge Underwood, J. M. Botts, Mayor Chahoon of Richmond, Mayor Burgess of Petersburg, General Williams C. Wickham, General Mulford, Franklin Stearns and others.[15]

The summer and fall months of 1868 wore on without any great political events in Virginia. Radical orators continued the campaign among the negroes and the latter were more hopeful and aspiring than ever. It was the golden age

---

[14] Congressional Globe, July 24, 1868, p. 4416: Beck's speech, "The real object of men who manipulated and projected this bill is to put all power into the hands of a few ultra radical leaders in that convention, and to deprive of the rights of suffrage twenty-five thousand white men in that State. The present provisional governor of Virginia, General Wells, came before the reconstruction committee and said . . . that in the first place he wanted a liberal appropriation to carry on the election. He wanted no further registration because, as he said, there were to-day twenty-five thousand white men in the State of Virginia, who under the present reconstruction laws, are entitled to be registered and vote, and if registered they would carry the State against the Republican party."

[15] Washington Star, quoted by Fredericksburg News, December 7, 1868.

of the colored race politically.[16] Meanwhile the whites had not emerged from their former apathy. The newspapers counselled the people to maintain an attitude of passive resistance, of stoical resignation. Many hoped that the Republican party might be defeated in the national election and the South thereby be saved. The Richmond Whig almost alone urged the acceptance of negro suffrage as inevitable, but its voice did not carry persuasion.[17] Yet this attitude was full of danger. The fall election resulted in a great Republican victory. General Grant was elected President and a large Republican majority was returned in the House of Representatives. Negro suffrage had, therefore, become an assured fact. The people opposed it as obstinately as ever, but a few thoughtful men in the conservative ranks realized the hopelessness of continuing the struggle against a sentiment that had grown into a sort of faith. There was also a danger that the Underwood constitution might be passed and the disfranchisement of a large class of citizens become a settled condition.

The Virginia constitution was brought up for the consideration of Congress early in the session, without opposition from the State. An effort was made to induce the conservative committees in Richmond to protest against the passage of an act approving the constitution, but they refused to stir in the matter.[18] The House of Representatives, on December 8, 1868, passed a bill which provided for an election on the Underwood constitution on the fourth Thursday in May, 1869.[19] The bill was then referred to the Senate, but before it could be acted upon Congress adjourned for the Christmas recess.

In this crisis Alexander H. H. Stuart came to the front. He had long enjoyed a high reputation in state and national affairs, having held the position of a Cabinet minister under

---

[16] Fredericksburg News, April 2, 1868.
[17] Whig, Novembe1 14, 1868.
[18] A. H. H. Stuart's "Restoration of Virginia," p. 18.
[19] Congressional Globe, 1868-9, p. 37.

Fillmore. Therefore he was well fitted for his statesmanlike but highly unpopular course of action. On December 25, 1868, an article on the political situation, written by Mr. Stuart under the signature of "Senex," appeared in both the Richmond Whig and the Richmond Dispatch. It commented with clearness upon the condition and needs of Virginia. Senex declared that it was quite useless for the people to resist the almost universal sentiment of the North in favor of negro suffrage. If Virginia would yield that point, she might possibly gain the removal of the disfranchising articles of the new constitution. Far better to accept negro suffrage, accompanied by the removal of disfranchisement, than have it forced on her with a continued disfranchisement. "Is it not better to surrender half than lose all? The Southern people had already made concessions, such as passing the constitutional amendment, abolishing slavery, and granting the blacks the right to testify in the courts, and neither of these measures had been followed by disastrous consequences. It would probably be likewise in the case of negro suffrage. The intelligence and the wealth of the South would continue to govern as before."[20]

In this article, "Senex," created a profound impression, or rather sensation. It met the strong disapproval of almost the entire conservative press; indeed it required some courage to advocate the acceptance of negro suffrage, even when the advocate was so well known and esteemed as Mr. Stuart. The great power of social proscription had been exerted to preserve the unity of the white race in the conservative party. Men who became active Republicans incurred the danger of ostracism. One radical orator pathetically declared that he had fought for four years in the Confederate army, but since he had joined the republican party, his own relatives would not recognize him.[21] The people had hitherto persisted in silent non-acquiescence in the reconstructive measures and they were not in haste to change

---

[20] "Restoration of Virginia," p. 22. [21] Enquirer, December, 1868.

their attitude. The newspapers criticized Stuart sharply. "For our own part," said the Enquirer, "we are unable to perceive any method of giving permanent peace to the country which does not recognize the absolute and essential inequality of the negro race as a basis of adjustment." [22]

Having thus prepared the way for discussion, Stuart, together with T. J. Michie, Judge H. W. Sheffey, N. K. Tront, J. B. Baldwin and several other conservative leaders, issued invitations for a conference to some of the prominent men of the State. The meeting was held in Richmond on December 31, 1868. Twenty-eight of the forty men invited were present. A. H. H. Stuart presided and C. C. MacRae acted as secretary.[23] A committee was appointed to go to Washington and make known to Congress the willingness of the members of the conference to accept negro suffrage, and to seek to obtain the best possible terms in regard to a constitution. The committee included A. H. H. Stuart, chairman, John L. Marye, Jr., James T. Johnston of Bedford, W. T. Sutherlin of Danville, Wyndham Robertson of Washington county, William L. Owen of Halifax, John B. Baldwin, James Neeson of Richmond and J. F. Slaughter of Lynchburg. These men have become known in Virginia history as the "Committee of Nine." The report of the committee declared that "the undersigned are prepared, and they believe the majority of the people of Virginia are prepared to surrender their opposition to its incorporation into their fundamental law as an offering on the altar of peace, and in the hope that union and harmony may be restored on the basis of universal suffrage and universal amnesty." General Stoneman expressed himself as in sympathy with the plan.

The movement of the committee of nine at once attracted the support of independent newspapers, such as the Richmond Whig,[24] and the strong opposition of the ultra-con-

---

[22] January 5, 1869 [23] The Enquirer, January 5, 1869.
[24] The Whig, January 7, 1869.

servative press led by the Enquirer. The latter exerted its great influence for the defeat of the committtee. In the conservative party many prominent leaders opposed the nine, among them ex-Governor Wise, R. T. Daniel, the chairman of the State committee, ex-Governor William Smith, Robert Ould and others. G. W. Bolling, James A. Seddon, Thomas S. Flournoy, Frank C. Ruffin, Judge Meredith, D. C. De Jarnette and Allan T. Caperton were some of the prominent conservatives who favored the committee.[25]

In Washington and the North the new movement attracted great attention. Early in January the New York Tribune began to lend its support, an accession of the very greatest importance.[26] Senators Stewart, Wilson, Howard, Sherman, Ross, Cole, Conkling were reputed to favor the efforts of the committee,[27] and all of the Democratic Congressmen, particularly Senators Hendricks of Indiana and Davis of Kentucky, and Representatives Beck and Brooks.[28] The committee of nine also received assistance from many other persons, among them D. C. De Jarnette, Gilbert C. Walker, Jonas Walker, Fayette McMullen, G. W. Bolling, R. H. Austin and L. Q. Washington, of the National Intelligencer. The services of Gilbert C. Walker were especially useful on account of his influence with General Rawlins and Senator Stewart.

The nine applied for permission to present their propositions before committees of the House of Representatives and of the Senate. At the same time two Republican committees came from Richmond to Washington to observe the movements of the conservative delegation.[29] One was unofficial and was composed of Franklin Stearns, Edgar Allan, L. H. Chandler and William Forbes, all prominent Republicans more or less conservative in their views. H.

---

[25] Richmond Whig, January 13, 1869.
[26] New York Tribune, January 14, 1869.
[27] New York Tribune, January 11, 1869.
[28] Richmond Whig, January 19, 1869.
[29] "Restoration of Virginia," p. 35.

H. Wells headed the other and official committee, containing both whites and blacks and favoring the adoption of the Underwood constitution without amendment. It was agreed that all three bodies should appear before the reconstruction committee to urge their various claims.

The first meeting was held on January 21. Colonel John B. Baldwin ably presented the argument of the committee of nine. He affirmed that the Virginia people were willing to accept universal suffrage, if reasonable concessions should be made to them. The committee of nine, he said, did not claim to represent any party, but the members were convinced that they received the support of a majority of Virginians. The nine proposed to consult and respect in the organic law of Virginia the decision of the country and the policy of the government concerning negro suffrage. It would be false to say that they favored negro suffrage, as, in their opinion, the admission of 450,000 blacks to the privilege of voting was a fearful experiment; yet, nevertheless, they accepted the policy of the Federal government in good faith.[30] Wells spoke next, stating that the one hope for justice to all classes in Virginia lay with the republican party, and that party alone could restore the State to prosperity.[31]

The reconstruction committee held several other sessions, at which the proposition of the nine was considered and evidence taken upon the condition of Virginia. Edwin Dudley, one of Wells's chief supporters, appeared in opposition to the committee of nine.[32] Editor Whittlesey, of the Virginia State Journal, the chief radical newspaper, testified to cases of outrages inflicted upon radicals. The Rev. Mr. Elder declared that the state of society in Virginia was little short of anarchy. On the other hand, Judge Sheffey[33] defended his assailed record and expressed his desire to do

[30] "Restoration of Virginia," p. 37.
[31] "Restoration of Virginia," p. 37.
[32] New York Tribune, January 27, 1869.
[33] New York Tribune, January 28.

justice to the colored race in his court; Judge Thomas also stated that he was free from political bias in his judicial work. A very important witness was the Republican politician, Lewis McKenzie, who favored the re-enfranchisement of Confederates. Baldwin was again of great service, particularly in controverting the adverse criticism of Whittlesey upon the Virginia courts and the vagrant and labor-contract acts.[34] After appearing before the reconstruction committee, the nine presented their plan to the judiciary committee of the Senate. Baldwin, as before, was the principal speaker.[35] An effort was also made to interest General Grant in the work of the nine, for his assistance as President would be indispensable. The committee in two interviews explained the objectionable features of the Underwood constitution and the objects of the new movement. Grant expressed his disapproval of "test-oaths" and disfranchisement, and also condemned the system of county organization in strong terms.[36]

The nine remained in the capital some days, to continue the agitation for the amendment of the Underwood constitution. The committee, chiefly through the conservative Republican delegation and through friends, such as the Walkers and Washington, brought a considerable influence to bear upon the ruling powers. It had done a great work, at least in promoting a more conciliatory feeling in Congress and also in the State; but there was no evidence of any immediate result commensurate with its purposes. Indeed, to many friends and enemies it seemed that the committee's

---

[34] Ibid., January 29 and 30. Baldwin's statement constitutes a strong defense of these much-abused laws.

[35] Baldwin prepared a statement of the committee's case for the judiciary committee. The obnoxious clauses of the constitution were Article III, Section 1, Paragraph 4, relating to disfranchisement; Article III, Section 7 and Section 3, which disqualified Confederates for office-holding and jury-service; Article IX, relating to church property; Article XI, containing a liberal homestead exemption and Article VIII, which made the public school system dependent upon local administration.

[36] "Restoration of Virginia," p. 46.

effort had failed;[37] and we may well believe that the result hung some time in doubt. February slowly dragged away and Congress took no action in reference to the petition of the nine. The nine finally succeeded, and the great service they rendered Virginia is well known; it was largely through their courageous and at first thankless endeavors that the State secured the unique opportunity which saved her from the worst evils of the reconstruction; but it must not in justice be forgotten that the Republicans who allied themselves to the conservative committee made success possible. The most distinguished men in the Republican party in Virginia aided the nine and their influence in a critical time probably proved decisive. Almost certainly the Federal government would not have made concessions, if the Republicans of Virginia had united in opposing them. After the committee of nine had left Washington and while the issue of its mission remained uncertain, Baldwin, with George Rye, Edgar Allan, L. H. Chandler and Wm. Forbes, returned and again urged that Virginia should be allowed to vote upon the disfranchising and test-oath articles of the constitution separately.[38] For some time no action was taken by the Federal government concerning the proposition of the committe of nine. Meanwhile the political situation in Virginia had greatly changed. The barriers between liberal conservatives and liberal Republicans were largely broken down. Men of both parties worked together to amend the Underwood constitution and to bring Virginia back to her Federal relations. The press of the State was widely divided. The Enquirer maintained its attitude of uncompromising hostility towards the acceptance of negro

[37] Enquirer, February 22: "We very humbly ask our neighbors of the Whig and Dispatch whether they think now that the 'new movement' has accomplished anything." To which the Whig of February 24 replied: "We do not doubt that the committee which went to Washington did service there in creating a better feeling among members of Congress." It will be seen that the Whig was not particularly sanguine. Also see the Whig, February 6 and 19.

[38] General Edgar Allan's Scrap-book.

suffrage, and the Enquirer was the most influential paper in Virginia. Against it were arrayed the Richmond Whig and the Richmond Dispatch, together with other leading journals. Several well-known papers remained neutral.[39]

The division within the Republican party had grown into a serious schism. The chief cause of factional disagreement was the personality and conduct of H. H. Wells, Governor of Virginia and the recognized head of the party. He had made it evident that he was willing to allow the State to come under negro domination, in order to win an election to the governorship, which knowledge alienated the leading Republicans of conservative temper. Other politicians opposed Wells for personal reasons; perhaps his preference for certain friends had made against him with the more neglected leaders. Furthermore, Wells had incurred the hostility of General William Mahone, who, as the leading railroad man of Virginia, exerted a considerable influence.

The opposition to the leadership of Wells finally grew to such an extent that it was proposed to hold another convention and make new nominations for the Republican party. The State executive committee, composed of Messrs. White, Douglas, Corprew, Platt, W. H. Samuel, H. G. Bond, Washburne, Oliver, Leahy, Forbes, Jenkins, Dudley, O. E. Hine, Henderlite and G. S. Smith, met in the last of January, set aside the nominations made in 1868, and issued a call for another convention to assemble in Petersburg in March.[40] Both factions worked energetically in the interval before the meeting of the new convention. The opponents of Wells wished to nominate in his place James H. Clements or L. H. Chandler, both of whom were prominent and influential. Willliam H. Samuel, George Rye, Edgar Allan and Charles W. Buttz led in this movement. But behind them and directing their energies for the downfall of Wells stood William Mahone.

[39] New York Tribune, January 14, 1869.
[40] Richmond Whig, January 30, 1869.

Mahone was the most remarkable man of later Virginia history. His career as a Confederate general in the closing months of the war had been brilliant. With the coming of peace he became a business man, and was finally elected to the presidency of the Virginia and Tennessee Railroad. Connected with this line were several smaller railways, and it was Mahone's purpose to consolidate them all into one strong westward-going system. It is said that Wells before his appointment as governor pledged himself to work for the merging of these railroads. But the Baltimore and Ohio Railroad was opposed to the re-election of Mahone as president of the consolidated system, a system which threatened to become, in energetic hands, an important rival for the western trade. On October 25, 1868, R. T. Wilson, an agent of the Baltimore and Ohio, arrived in Richmond, to work against the consolidation. He proposed to Wells that he should sell out the State's interest in the Virginia and Tennessee to the Baltimore and Ohio, a deal which would have been advantageous to the governor. Wells wished to accept the offer and sought George Rye, the State Treasurer, and a member of the Board of Public Works, in order to induce him to sanction the sale. This Rye refused to do, published the dangerous scheme and thereby defeated it. General Stoneman, who was also approached, also refused to lend consent.[41] The whole State was naturally stirred up over this plan to make Virginia a mere commercial tributary of Baltimore, and Wells, who had not been popular before, was now looked upon with dislike and distrust. Moreover, in winning the enmity of Mahone, the governor had brought into the field against him an exceedingly able and energetic politician. Mahone, although not a Republican at this time, at once began intriguing with the Republican leaders who were dissatisfied with Wells and working to have his renomination set aside.

Well's feud with Edgar Allan and W. H. Samuel also

---

[41] Norfolk Day-book, July 7, 1869.

originated in the previous year. Samuel was one of the first men to oppose the governor. In December, 1868, he wrote a letter to Allan, in which he set forth plans for defeating Wells for nomination. This letter, it seems, never reached Allan; at all events, it fell into the hands of Wells. Allan then charged the latter, together with his lieutenants, L. Edwin Dudley, H. G. Bond and C. E. Zincke, with stealing the letter from the mail.

It was under such conditions of bittter party strife that the time for the meeting of the Republican convention drew near. The anti-Wells faction was very active. Edgar Allan, Mahone's chief agent and one of the cleverest politicians in the State, established headquarters in Petersburg several days in advance of the convention, and, assisted by Samuel, Buttz, Norton and others, made every effort to win over the incoming delegates. Circulars attacking Wells were freely distributed, in which he was charged with the theft of the Samuel letter, with endeavoring to sell out Virginia's interests in the Virginia and Tennessee Railroad for his own profit,[42] and with complicity in the whiskey ring.

The convention, which met on the 9th of March, was one of the most turbulent and stormy in the history of the State. Opposition to Wells had grown to considerable extent; George Tucker, Luther Lee, Edgar Allan, Samuel, Maddox, Buttz, Leahy, Jackson, J. H. Painter and Dunbar were among the prominent men arrayed against him. But the Wells leaders, Bond, Platt, Dudley and Dr. Sharpe, commanded the support of the great majority of blacks. The first difficulty arose over the election of a chairman. After an exceedingly disorderly vote, George Tucker, the Clements candidate, was declared elected, but when he attempted to take his seat, the Wells delegates became riotous. Efforts of the police to restore order were not successful. Mayor Burgess then threatened to send for troops, and order

---

[42] Enquirer, March 11, 1869. Richmond Whig, March 10.

was finally restored, with the Wells party in control of the convention. The next day, after another tumultuous scene, permanent officers were elected—Orrin E. Hine, president; L. G. Bowden, Henry Williams (colored), John Page, Geo. Tucker, John Averett, Charles H. Lewis, J. J. Robertson, F. H. Johnson and W. P. Mosely, vice-presidents; and L. E. Dudley, George Timoh (colored), W. S. Fernand and J. R. Painter, secretaries.[43]

The selection of nominees was then in order. H. H. Wells again received the nomination for governor, without opposition, as it was evident that he controlled a majority of delegates. Apparently the fight against him had now come to an end, but while his enemies could not prevent his nomination, they were able to inflict injury upon him. For lieutenant-governor, the Wells leaders presented Dr. W. W. C. Douglass of Richmond county, a Confederate surgeon. A negro thereupon proposed the name of the colored Dr. Harris. Edgar Allan,[44] in order to thoroughly discredit the Wells ticket by forcing a negro upon it, seconded the nomination of Harris in an eloquent speech that completely won over the colored delegates. Harris was nominated, to the disgust of Wells and his supporters.

The nomination of Harris was a very clever move, for it unquestionably weakened the radical ticket. But that was still formidable from the support of the whole negro race and of many whites. Wells's chances of election were still very good. Consequently the men opposed to him determined to divide the Republican party.[45] After the adjournment of the convention, General Mahone and Edgar Allan, C. W. Buttz, J. W. Jenkins, W. H. Samuel, George Rye, D. B. White, Parsons and Segar met in room No. 8 of Jarrett's Hotel, and decided to place another ticket in the field. Gilbert C. Walker was chosen for governor. He had, indeed, all the qualifications for the peculiar position he was to oc-

[43] Richmond Whig, March 11.
[44] Statement of Edgar Allan, and Richmond Whig, March 12, 1869.
[45] Statement of General Allan.

cupy as the candidate of the moderate Republicans. He was a Republican, but strongly opposed the proscriptive features of the Underwood constitution, and had rendered the committee of nine conspicuous aid in their efforts for the restoration of the State. He was, therefore, well fitted to become a compromise candidate.

An address was published presenting the new Republican nominees—Gilbert C. Walker for governor, John F. Lewis for lieutenant-governor, and James C. Taylor for attorney-general;[46] this was signed by Franklin Stearns, Horace L. Kent, George Rye, Edgar Allan, G. K. Gilmer, J. W. Hunnicutt, Charles H. Lewis, John S. Devlin, and about one hundred and fifty other prominent Republicans.[47] They styled themselves the "True Republican" party, as opposed to the followers of Wells, and sent Edgar Allan to Washington as a representative.[48]

The conservative party made no new nominations. It was indeed in a state of considerable distraction. Some conservatives favored the plan of the committee of nine, but the great majority still strongly opposed any compromise.[49]

But however conservatives might differ as to the committee of nine, Republicans were far more and irreconcilably divided. The antagonism to Wells went so far that on March 23, the governor, H. G. Bond, register in bankruptcy, and Edward Dudley, clerk of the circuit court, were brought before the United States commissioner, Mayor Chahoon, in Richmond, on a warrant issued by Edgar Allan and W H. Samuel, charging them and C. E. Zincke with the theft of the former's letter.[50] It was not proven, however, that the letter was stolen and the case was dismissed, but Wells had seen and used the letter and had thereby become implicated in a very discreditable business. This and the other charges made against him by members

[46] Enquirer, March 11, 1869. [47] "Restoration of Virginia," p. 53.
[48] Edgar Allan's Scrap-book.
[49] Fredericksburg News, April 26, 1869. [50] Whig, March 24.

of his own party did not tend to enhance his reputation and increase his popularity with the people of Virginia. On March 28, General Stoneman, without assigning a reason, deposed Wells from the governorship. This action was taken, it is said, on account of Wells's free use of the pardoning power. A few days later Stoneman reappointed him to his office, where he remained until near the end of the reconstruction.

The result of the efforts of the committee of nine and of allied Republicans now became evident. President Grant on April 7, 1869, sent his first message to Congress, in which he recommended that the Underwood constitution should be submitted to a popular vote for ratification or rejection, and that a separate vote should be taken upon the adoption or rejection of such sections of the constitution as might seem expedient.[51] On April 10, Congress passed a bill providing that the President might choose a time for submitting the constitution to the vote of the people; and might also have a separate vote taken upon such provisions of it as he deemed best, the vote to be upon each clause apart or upon them all together.[52] In accordance with this act, President Grant issued a proclamation on May 14, appointing July 6, 1869, as the day for the election and ordering a separate vote upon Article III, Section I, Clause 4, and Article III, Section VII, the disfranchising and "test-oath" clauses respectively. The article concerning the new method of local organization was not submitted, on account, it seems, of the fear of some members of the cabinet that the people of Virginia wished to secure this amendment in order to avoid the establishment of public schools.[53] This exception stirred up a good deal of indignation in the State, for the people had come to believe that the "county organization" clause would be included with the other two. Yet the important concessions

[51] Messages and Papers of the Presidents, VII, 11.
[52] Code of Virginia (1873), p. 26.
[53] "Restoration of Virginia," p. 57. Macpherson's Scrap-book of the Campaign of 1869, Vol. I, p. 42.

had been won in gaining the right to vote upon the proscriptive measures apart from the constitution.

The political situation in Virginia was now complicated. Three parties were in the field. The conservative nominees, headed by Colonel Withers, uncompromisingly opposed the Underwood constitution. Governor Wells and the radicals favored the adoption of the constitution without any change whatever. Lastly, the conservative Republican party, with its gubernatorial candidate, Gilbert C. Walker, desired the amendment of the Underwood constitution by omitting the disfranchising and the "test-oath" articles. The contest would evidently lie between the conservative and radical parties, for the great body of white people were conservatives and the negroes almost entirely radical. The few conservative Republicans could hope to do little as a separate party.

The conservatives had a small advantage in number, but the colored vote was more compact and would likely be delivered almost as a unit. Furthermore, Mr. Stuart says that the conservative leaders feared that Governor Wells would be "counted in," whichever way the election might go.[54] In this dilemma the executive committee of the conservative party issued a call for a convention to decide upon the best course to pursue. As before, in the election of the Walker ticket, William Mahone was behind the movement to a considerable extent. As the leading railroad man of the State, Mahone occupied an extraordinary position and had weight with both parties. He now used his influence with the chairman of the conservative committee, R. T. Daniel, and with other members, particularly Robert Ould, to further what had been for some time desired by the moderate leaders—the withdrawal of the conservative ticket from the field. Besides Mahone, the committee of nine, unpartisan and sensible of the probability of Wells's election under the existing circumstances, gave their strong support to the move-

[54] "Restoration of Virginia," p. 52.

ment for fusion with the Walker party. The influence of the leading man of the nine, John B. Baldwin, was especially great and did much to aid the plan.

The convention met at Richmond on April 28, 1869.[52] R. T. Daniel presided. The nominees of the party, Colonel Withers, General Walker and John L. Marye, Jr., formally presented their resignations. A long discussion followed. The majority, led by John R. Edmunds, John B. Baldwin, Colonel Randolph, Robert Ould and R. T. Daniel favored the acceptance of the resignations and union with the conservative Republicans. The opposition also contained strong men—Ex-Governor William Smith, James Barbour, B. H. Shackelford, John Goode, Jr.,[56] and General Kemper. The convention adopted the majority report of the committee on business, which was signed by Robert Ould, John B. Baldwin, John L. Edmunds, Fayette McMullen, L. B. Anderson, James C. Campbell, A. Moseley, W. D. Haskins, W. T. Sutherlin. By this report the resignations of the candidates were accepted; no other men were nominated in their places, and the convention, while expressing its opposition to the objectionable features of the Underwood constitution, made no recommendation as to whom the conservative voters should support. The minority report of John Goode, Jr., Hugh Latham and J. G. Mason declared that the clauses of the constitution which were to be submitted to a separate vote for expurgation were immaterial in view of the leading measures of that constitution—"negro suffrage and negro eligibility to office."

The action of the convention meant fusion with the conservative Republican party. There were now but two State tickets in the field—those of Wells and Walker—and between these two it was easy for conservative voters to choose. But the movement towards the support of Walker was rather slow. A large part of the press still held out against com-

---

[55] Enquirer and Whig, April 29, 1869.

[56] President of the Virginia Constitutional Convention of 1901-2.

promise.[57] The Enquirer and many other papers refused to yield. However, an address of the State executive committee of the conservative party, published through Virginia in the first days of June, strengthened the fusion sentiment. This address explained the changed attitude of the national government towards the State and the opportunity offered the white race to regain control of affairs by accepting the Underwood constitution with the obnoxious clauses expurgated. In order to best accomplish this purpose, it was recommended that conservatives should unite in supporting Gilbert C. Walker.[58]

This out-and-out endorsement of Walker by the conservative leaders produced the desired effect. The conservatives now joined the Walker party almost as a man. The fusion became complete and conservative Republicans were supported for the legislature by the conservatives in many districts. But in view of the preponderance of the latter element, a great majority of the legislative nominees of the party were conservatives. The campaign became exceedingly active, one of the most active and exciting that Virginia has ever seen. The Union Leagues had gone to pieces in many places from threats of the farmers not to employ laborers who were members; the strongest pressure was brought to bear upon the blacks in the endeavor to detach them from the radical party. While the great majority of negroes stood firm, some impression was made upon their strength. Many old Republican leaders such as Edgar Allan, now supported Walker and exerted an important influence among the blacks. Furthermore, in order to gain colored votes, the conservatives nominated several negroes for the legislature, a device which worked well. Many employers threatened to discharge their colored workmen, if they voted the Wells ticket.[59] The apathy of the conserva-

[57] Fredericksburg News, June 16, 1869.

[58] Fredericksburg News, June 3, 1869.

[59] Washington Chronicle, quoted by the Fredericksburg News, July 12, 1869.

tive party had vanished in the rising hope that the reconstruction now drew near the end. On the other hand, the radicals were by no means inactivé. Although deserted by many former party leaders, Wells directed his campaign with ability and energy; he traveled through the State and drew great crowds of negroes with his eloquence. Wells had at first supported the disfranchising and "test-oath" clauses, but when he saw the overwhelming adverse sentiment, he declared his opposition to them, though leaving adoption or rejection an open question for the voters.

The election was held on July 6, 1869. It resulted in the victory of Gilbert C. Walker, who received 119,535 votes to 101,204 cast for H. H. Wells. Walker's majority was, therefore, 18,331.[60] Both clauses of the constitution submitted to a separate vote were defeated, the disfranchising article by a vote of 124,360 to 84,410; the "test-oath" clause by a vote of 124,715 to 83,458. The constitution was adopted.

No new name could conceal the fact that the election was a great conservative triumph. While the governor-elect was a moderate Republican, the fruits of victory remained almost entirely with the former party. The difference between the Walker Republicans and the conservatives was fundamental. The conservative (or Walker) Republicans regarded negro suffrage as a political principle, the conservative party, as a necessary evil. The legislature contained a very large conservative majority, no less than seventy in a body of 180 members. Twenty-seven negroes were elected, three of them conservatives. The great majority in the legislature insured the entire control of the State by that party.

Now that the victory was gained, General Canby threatened to dash it away. He had succeeded Stoneman in command of the district on April 20, 1869.[61] On April 22, he issued an order declaring that all State officers would be required to take the "test-oath;" and on May 7 he ordered

---

[60] It will be noted that a difference of slightly over 9,000 would have changed the result.

[61] Appleton's Annual Cyclopædia, 1869, p. 710.

all persons who had taken the oath to file a notice of the fact at headquarters, on pain of losing their offices in case of disobedience. Furthermore, on June 26, he announced that members of the legislature would have to take the oath, unless the constitution should first be approved by Congress, "or the oath be otherwise dispensed with by law." [62] This statement caused great fear among the conservatives, as many members of the assembly could not subscribe to the "test-oath." A. H. H. Stuart thereupon appealed to President Grant against General Canby's proposed action. Apparently his letter was effectual, for the President commanded Canby to withdraw the order.[63] But even after the election the latter re-asserted his views. He wrote to the New York Times that he would have suspended the meeting of the legislature until the constitution had been approved by Congress if Congress had not directed that it should meet at a definite time. As that was the case, it would be his duty to enforce the law concerning the "test-oath," until it was repealed. The United States Attorney-General, on August 28, decided that the members of the assembly might meet and facilitate the restoration of the State without taking the oath, but could not go into any "general legislation." [64]

Accordingly the legislature came together on October 5, 1869.[65] Before the meeting Governor Wells, seeing that his political career in Virginia had ended, resigned his office. Gilbert C. Walker was then inaugurated on September 21. When the assembly met the radical members protested against any State officer entering upon his duties without taking the "test-oath." In the senate on October 6, a resolution to that effect was laid on the table. Finally the useless opposition came to an end.

The two new amendments to the Constitution of the United States were ratified on October 8; the fourteenth by a vote of 36 to 4 in the Senate and 126 to 6 in the house

---

[62] Appleton's Annual Cyclopædia, 1869, p. 713.
[63] "Restoration of Virginia," p. 67.
[64] Appleton's Annual Cyclopædia, 1869, p. 713.
[65] Enquirer, October 6.

of delegates; the fifteenth by a vote of 40 to 2 in the senate, and unanimously in the house.[66] Virginia had now complied with the requirements demanded for restoration to the rights of statehood. A bill providing for the admission of representatives from Virginia passed Congress and was approved by the President on January 26, 1870. On the following day General Canby issued an order which resigned the government of the State to the civil authorities.

The reconstruction of Virginia had come to an end after well-nigh five years of weary waiting. Nearly nine years had passed since the State had withdrawn her representation from the Federal Congress. After this long period of war and of political subjection the white people of Virginia now regained control of affairs. The reconstruction had for its ultimate purposes proven a failure. For it was the desire of Congress and the aim of the radical politicians in Virginia to place the two races on an equality of rights and privileges—to abolish the belief of the white man in the essential inferiority of the black. They thought that a democracy should no more recognize racial distinctions than real class distinctions. And so they had endeavored with motives high and low to break down the separation of the races. It was impossible that any such attempt should succeed. But reason was lost in the humanitarian enthusiasm of the times. Men had such faith in the power of literary education that they thought it could raise, in a day, the black folk to the level of the white. The radicals indeed gained the privilege of suffrage for the freedmen, but it remained purely isolated. The negro might not hold office, serve on juries and exercise the other political functions of citizens. There were no actual prohibitions of these things to the colored people, but a general agreement existed among the conservative whites that they should not enjoy them. And the white men have used all the devices of politics to prevent the local supremacy of the blacks in portions of the State where they held the majority.

---

[66] The Enquirer, October 9, 1867.

The results of the reconstruction were important for the negro. He was thereby assured of his emancipation from the influences as well as from the actual legal system of slavery, and of his separation from the white race. He gained the right to vote and the means to educate his children. He also suffered evils; for the radical politicians inspired an ignorant and generally contented race with alluring and quite impossible hopes. They awakened desires in the colored race which could not then be attained and which left a fruit of desolating discontent. Some of the radical leaders were men of high purpose, fine enthusiasts in the great cause of human rights, and faced abuse and ostracism in the course of their conceived duty but many of them endeavored to gain power for their own uses through a peculiarly dangerous form of demagogism.

The concurrence of the conservatives in negro suffrage was politically wise from a party standpoint, for the colored vote only once since the reconstruction has put the Republican party in power. In the "readjuster" movement in 1879 and the early eighties the republican and readjuster parties united and elected a governor and two United States Senators, but the Democratic party soon rallied and regained control. After that the best that the Republicans could do was to elect an occasional Congressman.

The recognition of negro suffrage, wrung from the reluctant white people, never grew into a belief in the wisdom and justice of that measure. Indeed a desire arose in the State to debar the negro as far as possible, from exercising his privilege of voting. The result is to be seen in the constitution of 1902 under which the great majority of blacks have been disfranchised through the educational and property qualifications which now hedge about the ballot in Virginia.